# *Buddha Root Farm*

# Buddha Root Farm

## Pure Land Talks

Dharma talks delivered by the

### *Venerable Master Hsuan Hua*

English translation by the
Buddhist Text Translation Society

Buddhist Text Translation Society
Dharma Realm Buddhist University
Dharma Realm Buddhist Association
Burlingame, California U.S.A.

*Buddha Root Farm - Pure Land Talks*

**Published and translated by:**

**Buddhist Text Translation Society**
1777 Murchison Drive, Burlingame, CA 94010-4504

© 2003   **Buddhist Text Translation Society**
**Dharma Realm Buddhist University**
**Dharma Realm Buddhist Association**

First edition 1976
Second edition 2003

11 10 09 08 07 06 05 04 03 02     10 9 8 7 6 5 4 3 2 1

ISBN 0-88139-432-7

Printed in Malaysia.

Addresses of the Dharma Realm Buddhist Association branches are listed at the back of this book.

Library of Congress Cataloging-in-Publication Data

Hsuan Hua, 1908-
  Buddha root farm : pure land talks : dharma talks / delivered by the Ven. Hsuan Hua.
    p. cm.
Translated from Chinese.
  ISBN 0-88139-432-7 (Soft : alk. paper)
  1. Pure Land Buddhism.  I. Title.
  BQ4535 .H76 2003
  294.3'444--dc21
                                                        2002002197

# Contents

# Introduction One

*"Of the colors of the mountains,*
*none are not his vast, long tongue;*
*In the sparkling streams and the forests green*
*his compassionate song is sung... "*

The lines above are descriptive of the Buddha Recitation Samadhi, a samadhi obtained through the single-minded concentration on the name of Amitabha Buddha. In a former life, Amitabha Buddha was a cultivator, a bhikshu named Dharma Treasury, and he made forty-eight vows, each one of which was to take living beings who recited his name to his Land of Ultimate Bliss, where they might cultivate and quickly become Buddhas.

In August 1975, a group of hard-working cultivators gathered at Buddha Root Farm to recite the Buddha's name. The Venerable Master Hua, Abbot of Gold Mountain Monastery in San Francisco, gave talks twice daily, elucidating the practice of Buddha Recitation.

It is said that the Buddha spoke all dharmas merely in the response to the needs of living beings. The Venerable Master's lectures also demonstrate this principle. In this volume you will watch the Master's skill extend from teaching the principle of compassion through the act of signing a peace-treaty with the mosquitoes on the mountain, to explaining the origin of humankind and the universe, to setting forth the principles of cause and effect, and other important Buddhist concepts, in a way that one can readily understand and readily identify. The Master has often said, "There are no fixed dharmas. There is no fixed way to explain the Dharma. If there were a fixed way to explain it, it would be a dead dharma, and the Dharma is not dead, it is *alive*."

The world abounds with theories and methods. People try with varying degrees of success to fit themselves into these "methods" in order to improve themselves. But the teaching of a true master, a genuine Knowing Advisor, is without theory, without method. His teaching is like a spotless mirror, always ready to reflect, always responding with a teaching which is exactly appropriate to the needs of the disciple, showing the disciple how to become free from attachments, and eventually realize enlightenment.

The presence of such a teacher in the world is not a common occurrence by any means.

How different it was to sit still and to contemplate the Buddha's name beside the winding river, with the yellow grasses, the wild flowers, and the host of forest creatures taking part! Indeed a contrast to the daily sound of life in the heart of San Francisco's Mission District where Gold Mountain Monastery is located. But was it, really? The fundamental teaching of the Buddhadharma is non-attachment. Cultivation in one place differs not in essence from cultivation in any other place…

In these days of environmental decay, one grows anxious for the future of our planet. Yet, the world we live in can never be more than a reflection of the state of our own hearts and minds. The Sutras say, "If the mind is pure, the Buddhaland is pure." If the mind is pure, if the heart is cleansed, the world, in turn, will be pure.

How does one purify the mind? This work, called cultivation, is the most difficult and yet the most rewarding job there is. It means eradicating the sources of defilement within us, casting out greed, hatred, and delusion and replacing them with morality, samadhi, and wisdom. The Buddhas have taught eighty-four thousand methods of doing just this very thing. To attempt to clean up the world while ignoring the pollution in one's own mind is a hopeless task.

Throughout the ages it has been those of higher vision, the saints and sages who have transcended the forces of evil within themselves, who have succeeded in exerting a lasting positive influence on humankind. An effort to reform society which is not coupled with an equal effort to develop one's spiritual self cannot bring about lasting results. It is like trying to cool a pot of boiling soup by merely stirring it, while ignoring the blazing fuel underneath.

One of the simplest yet most subtle methods of cultivation is that of Buddha Recitation. Single-minded concentration on the Buddha of Infinite Light can melt away karmic obstacles that would fill the entirety of empty space, and lead one directly back to the source of light within us. In the talks which follow, the Master explains these principles clearly. His words provided instruction and inspiration to those assembled at Buddha Root Farm, and they serve as a wealth of Dharma for cultivators of the future.

> *"...the water flows, the wind blows—*
> *whispering his name.*
> *And when he takes you by the hand to the Happy Land,*
> *You'll be so glad you came."*

**Bhikshuni Heng Yin**

*Translator*
*International Institute for the Translation of Buddhist Texts*
*San Francisco*
*February, 1976*

# Introduction Two

In the summer of 1975, as the Aquarian full moon approached, Bill Brevoort decided that the best way to honor the occasion would be by hosting a recitation session so that the name of Amitabha Buddha could echo through the hills and valleys, across the Smith River, and over the acres of Buddha Root Farm. With the idea firmly planted, he began preparation, which started with letters to Gold Mountain explaining his plan and respectfully requesting the Venerable Abbot and the Sangha and lay communities to join in the session. Having received acceptance, he set to work preparing the banks of the Smith River for the session.

Although publicity was limited, people came from all over the country to join in the session. More than fifty people participated daily in the session, and several dozen visitors came during the course of the week to learn about the Pure Land practice and join in the meditation.

This session on Buddha Root Farm marked the first time an orthodox Buddha Recitation Session had been conducted under open skies in the mountains. As the days progressed the sound of the chant became clear and harmonious and many who participated found their concentration deepening as they gained an understanding of the profound principles of the Dharma.

A circular path was cleared beside the main tent where members of the assembly circumambulated to the right as they chanted the name of Amitabha Buddha.

Meditation under the main tent brought a sense of "light ease" to more experienced participants and a chance to work on quieting the mind for all concerned. The half hour sitting meditation periods alternated with half hours of walking meditation while chanting aloud the name of Amitabha Buddha. An hour sit each evening from 5:30 to 6:30 was a popular part of the session and many guests who came for the evening lectures arrived early enough to join in the one long sit of the day. The large main tent provided ample cover from the hot afternoon sun and the downpours of rain which occurred during the week. The days began with the traditional morning recitation of mantras and sutras at 4:00am, followed by two hours of meditation.

The *Amitabha Sutra* was recited three times daily, in the early morning, after the noon meal, and late in the evening. Walking and sitting continued without interruption from 7:00 am until 10:30 am at which time the Great Meal Offering was made and all enjoyed a hearty meal, the meal which, for most of them, was their only meal of the day. The afternoons were filled with more chanting and sitting, a lively talk by a student of the Dharma, and a lecture by the Venerable Master. After the one hour meditation period in the evening, the evening recitation was held, followed by the second of the Master's daily lectures. Following the lecture, the Great Transference of Merit was held, and then the day was "complete" and finished.

The Master's lectures, here presented, included extensive question and answer periods. The Master brought the Pure Land Dharma-door alive as he explained the fundamentals of practice and revealed the fruits of cultivation. The Master spoke with such simplicity that even the most uninformed beginners could comprehend the principles, and yet the profundity of his words led even the most knowledgeable members of the assembly right into the realm of the ineffable, inconceivable, miraculous vastness of the Dharma Realm.

At the end of the week a refuge-taking ceremony was held and seventeen people, young and old, children and adults, took refuge with the Triple Jewel and bowed to the Venerable Master as their teacher. After taking refuge, everyone made the four vast vows:

*Living beings are boundless;*
*I vow to save them.*
*Afflictions are endless;*
*I vow to sever them.*
*Dharma-doors are limitless;*
*I vow to master them.*
*The Buddha Way is supreme;*
*I vow to realize it.*

**Bhikshuni Heng Ch'ih**

*Buddhist Text Translation Society*
*San Francisco*
*December, 1975*

# Introduction Three

On one hand it was just another group of Young Americans come together amid the blackberries and foggy drizzle of the Oregon coastal mountains.

On the other hand, the week-long gathering on the wooded banks of the Smith River's North fork was totally unique.

This conversation took place all across the land wherever friends met with those who had taken part.

"Who were those people?"

"They were all Americans: straights and hippies, locals and lawyers, mountain-folk, Harvard grads, voyagers, Ph.Ds., housewives, drop-outs, businessmen and surfers, poets and seekers of all sorts and ages. Some of the men and women wore rag-robes and had no hair. They were Buddhist monks and nuns."

"Sounds like an interesting group. What did they do that was so different?"

"There was no meat on the table, for one thing, no drugs, no alcohol, no frisbees, no fighting and no frenzy of any kind. If you simply watched them, you might have thought they weren't doing much of anything. They walked in circles day and night in the out-of-doors, now praying, now singing, now sitting quietly under a tarp tent. But if you knew what was really going on you might have said they were making a gentle but powerful revolution."

"That's an important word in America these days, what with the bicentennial year and all. How can you make revolution in the Oregon mountains?"

"The British historian Toynbee said that the kind of thing they did in their wilderness retreat will have an ultimate impact more significant to the social fabric of Western society than any other historical event in the Twentieth Century: bigger than the world wars, more important than the atom bomb, more far-reaching than space travel."

"That's some claim. What were they doing, then?"

"They were looking for Paradise."

"Big deal! I could get high too by heading for the mountains and leaving the evil in the cities behind... besides, a lot of groups in this country have tried to make Utopias, but they all fold after about twenty years. Isn't this just another fad?"

"Suppose I told you that groups exactly like this have met and practiced in this way for the past 3,000 years? This trip comes directly from Asia to the West."

"I'd say they were really together people."

"It's just that they have a *method* called Buddha Recitation, and Americans can dig it since you do it yourself. It's got three parts. First you have to believe that Paradise—the Pure Land—exists. Secondly, you have to break your bad habits, like drinking and eating meat. The idea is to stop harming yourself and other people. Thirdly, you promise yourself that you will do what it takes to get to the Pure Land, which is just applying the method. It's not an arbitrary whim of divine grace involved or a matter of chance. It's just that if you do the work, you succeed—100% democratic. And you shouldn't look outside of yourself for Paradise or postpone your real life, your real happiness, until you find that one spot on Earth that's better than some other spot. Instead, you live right where you are and by working inside with the method you turn your own space into Paradise. You can carry it with you. Once you truly realize it,

Paradise is permanent and portable. It's not limited to one object, one idea, one person, or one point in space or time."

"Wow! That's really different from anything I've heard before. You know, I've always been restless, anxious to move on and find a better place, but I'm tired of that now. I think maybe I'll stop right here and try this method. You say it really works?"

"Try it."

**Shramanera Heng Sure**

*Gold Mountain Monastery*
*San Francisco*
*February, 1976*

# The Venerable Master Hsuan Hua

## A Brief Portrait

"I have had many names," he once said, "and all of them are false." In his youth in Manchuria, he was known as "the Filial Son Bai"; as a young monk he was An Tzu ("Peace and Kindness"); later, in Hong Kong, he was Tu Lun ("Wheel of Rescue"); finally, in America, he was Hsuan Hua, which might be translated as "one who proclaims the principles of transformation." To his thousands of disciples across the world, he was always also "Shr Fu" – "Teacher."

Born in 1918 into a peasant family in a small village on the Manchurian plain, Master Hua was the youngest of ten children. He attended school for only two years, during which he studied the Chinese Classics and committed much of them to memory. As a young teenager, he opened a free school for both children and adults. He also began then one of his lifelong spiritual practices: reverential bowing. Outdoors, in all weathers, he would make over 800 prostrations daily, as a profound gesture of his respect for all that is good and sacred in the universe.

He was nineteen when his mother died, and for three years he honored her memory by sitting in meditation in a hut beside her grave. It was during this time that he made a resolve to go to America to teach the principles of wisdom. As a first step, at the end of the period of mourning, he entered San Yuan Monastery, took as his teacher Master Chang Chih, and subsequently received the full ordination of a Buddhist monk at Pu To Mountain. For ten years he devoted himself to study of the Buddhist scriptural tradition and to mastery of both the Esoteric and the Chan Schools of Chinese Buddhism. He had also read and contemplated the scriptures of Christianity, Taoism, and Islam. Thus, by the age of thirty, he had already established through his own experience the four major imperatives of his later ministry in America: the primacy of the monastic tradition; the essential role of moral education; the need for Buddhists to ground themselves in traditional spiritual practice and authentic scripture; and, just as essential, the importance and the power of ecumenical respect and understanding.

In 1948, Master Hua traveled south to meet the Venerable Hsu Yun, who was then already 108 years old and China's most distinguished spiritual teacher. From him Master Hua received the patriarchal transmission in the Wei Yang Lineage of the Chan School. Master Hua subsequently left China for Hong Kong. He spent a dozen years there, first in seclusion, then later as a teacher at three monasteries which he founded.

Finally, in 1962, he went to the United States, at the invitation of several of his Hong Kong disciples who had settled in San Francisco. By 1968, Master Hua had established the Buddhist Lecture Hall in a loft in San Francisco's Chinatown, and there he began giving nightly lectures, in Chinese, to an audience of young Americans. His texts were the major scriptures of the Mahayana. In 1969, he astonished the monastic community of Taiwan by sending there, for final ordination, two American women and three American men, all five of them fully trained as novices, fluent in Chinese and conversant with Buddhist scripture. During subsequent years, the Master trained and oversaw the ordination of hundreds of monks and nuns who came to California from every part of the world to study with him. These monastic disciples now teach in the 28 temples, monasteries and convents that the Master founded in the United States, Canada, and several Asian countries.

Although he understood English well and spoke it when it was necessary, Master Hua almost always lectured in Chinese. His aim was to encourage Westerners to learn Chinese, so that they could become translators, not merely of his lectures, but of the major scriptural texts of the Buddhist Mahayana. His intent was realized. So far, the Buddhist Text Translation Society, which he founded, has issued over 130 volumes of translation of the major Sutras, together with a similar number of commentaries, instructions, and stories from the Master's teaching.

As an educator, Master Hua was tireless. From 1968 to the mid 1980's he gave as many as a dozen lectures a week, and he traveled extensively on speaking tours. At the City of Ten Thousand Buddhas in Talmage, California, he established formal training programs for monastics and for laity; elementary and secondary schools for boys and for girls; and Dharma Realm Buddhist University, together with the University's branch, the Institute for World Religions, in Berkeley.

Throughout his life the Master taught that the basis of spiritual practice is moral practice. Of his monastic disciples he required strict purity, and he encouraged his lay disciples to adhere to the five precepts of the Buddhist laity. Especially in his later years, Confucian texts were often the subject of his lectures, and he held to the Confucian teaching that the first business of education is moral education. He identified six rules of conduct as the basis of communal life at the City of Ten Thousand Buddhas; the six rules prohibit contention, covetousness, self-seeking, selfishness, profiting at the expense of the community, and false speech. He asked that the children in the schools he had founded recite these prohibitions every morning before class. In general, although he admired the independent-mindedness of Westerners, he believed that they lacked ethical balance and needed that stabilizing sense of public morality which is characteristic of the East.

The Venerable Master insisted on ecumenical respect, and he delighted in inter-faith dialogue. He stressed commonalities in religious traditions – above all their emphasis on proper conduct, on compassion, and on wisdom. He was also a pioneer in building bridges between different Buddhist national traditions. He often brought monks from Theravada countries to California to share the duties of transmitting the precepts of ordination. He invited Catholic priests to celebrate the mass in the Buddha-Hall at the City of Ten Thousand Buddhas, and he developed a late-in-life friendship with Paul Cardinal Yu-Bin, the exiled leader of the Catholic Church in China and Taiwan. He once told the Cardinal: "You can be a Buddhist among the Catholics, and I'll be a Catholic among Buddhists." To the Master, the essential teachings of all religions could be summed up in a single word: wisdom.

### *Kuo Chou Rounds*

*Bodhisattva Precepts Disciple*
*Member, Buddhist Text Translation Society*

Participants file across a narrow boardwalk that spans the Smith River on their way to the tent. Everyone made this trip from the base camp to the tent at least six times a day!

Bill Brevoort, the owner of Buddha Root Farm and host of the Amitabha Session measures the ropes that form the structure for the canvas tent where participants will meditate, chant the Buddha's name, and listen to talks on the Pure Land Dharma.

Bhikshu Heng Su and Bhikshuni Heng Yin prepare to lead the assembly in chanting the Buddha's name.

Participants reciting in the Pure Land ceremony beneath the tent as part of the daily practice.

Venerable Master Hua talks to participants about Amitabha Buddha and his vows, and also gives practical instructions in how to recite the Buddha's name and sit in meditation. Question and answer periods were lively and informative.

Well-formed Chinese calligraphy adorns the yellow banner that spans the tent. The words read: Namo Amitabha Buddha!

The Master's talks were delightful and he enjoyed sharing the Pure Land practice with everyone.

Participants listen to Master Hua explain how to meditate, how to chant, and how to be good people.

Young American monks, nun, laymen, and laywomen take turns translating the Master's talks into English.

Participants make prostrations prior to taking refuge with the Triple Jewel: the Buddha, the Dharma, and the Sangha. Master Hua presides, offering those who wish, the opportunity to become Buddhists.

Each day's practice divides into a half-hour walking and chanting period, followed by a half-hour sitting and chanting period, followed by a half-hour silent sit. Here, participants are sitting silently under the shade of the tent.

Young Americans from the Oregon area gather here to listen to Master Hua teach them about Buddhism's fundamental principles, and to especially instruct them in the benefits of reciting Amitabha Buddha's name and of meditating.

The tent offered protection from the frequent rains and from the occasional hot sun. Its open sides allowed breeze to pass through, which helped send mosquitoes away unharmed!

The main meal was served around 11 am. Participants joined the meal ceremony in the tent and then filed down the hill and back across the Smith River boardwalk while reciting the Buddha's name. The noon meal – the only meal for the monastics – was served at the base camp. Bill's wife Peggie Brevoort prepared food that was both delicious and nutritious for the hungry cultivators.

# Everything's a test

## Sunday, August 17, 1975 (evening)

*Homage to the Eternally Dwelling Buddhas*
*of the Ten Directions*
*Homage to the Eternally Dwelling Dharma*
*of the Ten Directions*
*Homage to the Eternally Dwelling Sangha*
*of the Ten Directions*
*Homage to Our Teacher, Shakyamuni Buddha*
*Homage to the Shurangama*
*from the Buddha's Crown*
*Homage to the Bodhisattva*
*Who Observes the World's Sounds*
*Homage to the Vajra Treasury Bodhisattvas*

How are you? This Dharma Assembly is wonderful! Despite the rain, so many people have gathered here deep in the mountains to blaze trails through the wilderness. We are here to plant the seeds of Bodhi so that in the future we may harvest the fruit of Buddhahood.

What is meant by "planting the seeds of Bodhi?" Upasaka Bill has named this place "Buddha Root Farm." At Buddha Root Farm one should plant Bodhi seeds. First you plant a Bodhi seed, then you send down the Buddha Root, and in the future you will reap the

Buddha fruit. So your coming here is an extremely important first step.

Why do I say that it is important? Because if you recite the Buddha's name you can end birth and death, and then, like the Buddha, you can teach and transform living beings.

> *From limitless eons past*
> *Till now, each one of us*
> *Has been born and then died,*
> *Has died and been born*
> *Passed through birth upon birth—*
> *Death after death:*
> *Who knows how many times*
> *We've turned on the wheel?*

We have not yet encountered the Dharma-door of Buddha-recitation, and so we have not ended birth and death. Now, having learned the method of Buddha-recitation, we can be reborn in the Western Land of Ultimate Bliss. This is extremely important! Buddha-recitation is a serious matter because it can cause all living beings to end birth and death, gain release from the revolving wheel, separate from suffering, and attain bliss. Since it is so important, all of us participating here should be sincere, and recite with a true heart.

There's a way to determine if you are reciting with a true heart. If you are sincere, the mosquitoes will not bite you. If you are insincere, the mosquitoes *will* bite you. If you recite with a true heart, you won't be bothered by the rain. No matter how it pours, it won't dampen the mind which recites the Buddha's name. If you recite until

> *the wind blows, but doesn't touch you;*
> *the rain pours, but doesn't fall on you.*

If your only thoughts are to chant the Buddha's name, then it won't rain. The weather will be fine, that's certain. The mosquitoes won't bite you and the rain won't fall. These are some responses that come from sincere recitation of the Buddha's name. If you are simply pretending, then it will rain, the mosquitoes will bite, and you'll be miserable sitting there. If you recite well, however, even when the mosquitoes bite you'll pay no attention to them, and so it will be as if they hadn't bitten.

You should think, "I will endure the pain of being bitten. My only thought is to praise the Buddha's name. If the mosquitoes bite, I won't even know it." If you don't feel the bugs bite and if you don't know it's raining, that's being true-hearted. If your heart is sincere you will certainly have a special response. You may see Amitabha Buddha coming to rub you on the crown of your head or you may see him bathing you in light. Amitabha Buddha may appear and cover you with his sash. These are all responses:

> *His hand rubs my head,*
> *His sash covers me...*

Amitabha Buddha may respond in these ways.

So don't fear that the mosquitoes will bite. If you are unmoved by the rain, if you're not afraid to walk the rugged path back and forth, then your heart is true. If your heart is true, even when mosquitoes bite, you won't feel it. That's why I say they won't bite. They won't bite because you won't know that you have been bitten! If, as soon as a bug flies near you, you wince and think, "Oh no! Here comes a mosquito!" then you've forgotten about reciting.

This is not a joke. It's a very serious matter. When Kuo Yu said to me today that a mosquito had bitten him, I said, "You haven't been mindful and that's why the mosquito bit you." The mosquitoes are just acting on the principle that

*Everything's a test,*
*To see what you will do;*
*If you don't recognize*
  *what's before your eyes*
*You have to start anew!*

If you can't even push back the demonic obstacle of a mosquito, then you've really chanted the Buddha's name in vain.

That's all for today. I hope you all sleep well, and that the mosquitoes don't bite. If you recite as if you were asleep, then if the mosquitoes bite, you won't know it. When you're asleep you don't feel them bite; if you recite well, it's the same way.

# Namo Amitabha!

## Monday, August 18, 1975 (afternoon)

Today is the first full day of the Buddha Recitation Session. Those who have chanted the Buddha's name before know of its advantages. Those who have never recited before will not know what we are doing. "Namo, namo, namo – what?"

Amitabha!

"Well, what is Amitabha anyway?"

A Buddha!

"But what are we doing? We recite while we sit, recite while we walk, recite while we stand, and even when we lie down to sleep our minds are still reciting.What use is it?"

I will tell you:

> *To bow in worship before the Buddhas*
> *Eradicates offenses like the Ganges' sands.*

If you just bow once before the Buddhas, you eradicate as much bad karma as there are grains of sand in the River Ganges.

You say, "As grains of sand in the River Ganges? Well, I've sung the Buddha's name so many times, certainly my offense-karma has been completely wiped away."

You should be aware that from limitless eons ago, from the time when you first became a human being until the present, your incarnations are uncountable. You yourself may not even believe that you have past, present, and future lives. In each life you were confused, muddled and unclear, and therefore, at present, you don't know how much bad karma you have amassed as a human being. There is reason to fear that the bad deeds you have committed in one single life exceed the number of sand grains in the Ganges. Although reciting the Buddha's name will eradicate offense-karma like the Ganges' sands, you don't know how much of it exists. Fortunately, our bad deeds have no material form. If they did, each individual's karma would completely fill empty space. That's the extent of your offenses! But, because karma has no material form, empty space has yet to be filled. So it says,

> To bow in worship before the Buddhas
> Eradicates offenses like the Ganges' sands;
> To give a single penny
> Increases your blessings without limit.

In supporting the Bodhimanda, those with money give money. Those with strength give strength. Whether you give money or strength, the merit and virtue are the same, and they help you to plant good roots.

To recite the Buddha's name but once eradicates the grave offenses committed during ninety million eons of birth and death. In America, where the Buddhadharma is new, you now have the rare good fortune to encounter this method. What's more, you've met with a Good Advisor, one who can teach you the method of Buddha Recitation. No one should casually waste this precious time. Be very conscientious, work hard at your recitation, and you will not have attended the session in vain.

Here we are bivouacked out-of-doors under the open sky, camping in the wilds and reciting the Buddha's name. When it rains we recite beneath this big tarp. When the rain stops we recite while walking on a circular track. This is truly an excellent method! We have not come to this pure mountain land for sport or recreation, but only to recite the Buddha's name. This is truly a subtle, wonderful, and inconceivable environment. There are no sounds at all. It's not like San Francisco with its cars, buses, trolleys and planes going, "rrrrrrrr! rrrrrrrr!" – all making a tremendous din. It's very natural here, and perfect for Buddha Recitation. So all of you take care not to waste this precious time.

Deep in the mountains the air is fresh and there is not the slightest trace of pollution. The Five Turbid Evil Worlds – the Turbidity of the Eon, the Turbidity of Views, the Turbidity of Living Beings, the Turbidity of Afflictions, and the Turbidity of the Lifespan – exist in places crowded with people. This wilderness, by contrast, is the clear, pure Land of Ultimate Bliss. If you can cultivate in the Pure Land of Ultimate Bliss, the power of the response of the Way will be completely different from that of the noisy bustle of the city. Here, it is easy to enter samadhi, to gain concentration, to obtain the Buddha Recitation samadhi.

As you recite the Buddha's name:

*Every sound of the Buddha's name*
*is a sound of purity;*
*When every sound is recitation,*
*each thought is clear and pure.*
*When every thought is clear and pure*
*you obtain the Buddha Recitation samadhi.*

As it is said,

*One pure thought*
*is one thought of the Buddha.*
*When every thought is pure,*
*every thought is of the Buddha.*

Beside us runs a small river, and the sparkling water recites the Buddha's name. As you listen to it, it says, "Namo Amitabha Buddha." The blowing wind also recites the Buddha's name, proclaiming the wonderful Mahayana Dharma. This state is the same as that in the Land of Ultimate Bliss. In the Land of Ultimate Bliss:

*The water flows, the wind blows*
*Proclaiming the Mahayana;*
*In the pools of seven jewels*
*Are flowers of four colors*
*And waves of solid gold.*

The lotuses which bloom in the pools made of the seven jewels are green-colored of green light, yellow-colored of yellow light, red-colored of red light, white-colored of white light. Green, yellow, red, and white, the lights shine brightly.

You say, "Dharma Master, you have been explaining Buddha Recitation for quite a while now, but ultimately what is this 'namo, namo' all about? Namo what?"

"Namo" yourself! Don't "namo" anyone else. Think of it this way, "I have such good roots that I have learned to recite the Buddha's name!"

"Namo" means "to return my life and respectfully submit." This means to return your body, heart, and life and respectfully bow before Amitabha Buddha. Say to yourself, "I take my body, heart, and life and return in refuge to Amitabha Buddha."

You ask, "Well, if namo means to return the life and respectfully submit, what does 'Amitabha' mean? Can you explain that?"

Of course I can. Don't be nervous. I'll tell you in due time. If I don't finish this time, I'll continue next time. And if I don't finish next time, I'll continue later on. Don't worry. I am determined to teach you what "Namo Amitabha Buddha" is all about.

"Namo Amitabha" is Sanskrit. "Buddha" is also Sanskrit. "Amitabha" means "limitless light." Amitabha's other name, "Amitayus" means "limitless life." When you recite the Buddha's name, you obtain a limitless lifespan. Because you return your life and respectfully submit to the Buddha of Limitless Life, you may take the merit and virtue you obtain by reciting and live as long as you please!

If you say, "I want to live to be ninety-nine years old," then you will certainly not depart at age eighty-eight. You will live to be ninety-nine.

You say, "But I want to live to be a hundred!"

You can do that, too. All you need to do is recite the Buddha's name sincerely. This includes all of us gathered here today. I will now make a prediction: Those among you who want to live to a very old age will certainly get to do so. Not everyone, mind you, but only those who are sincere. Whoever recites sincerely will obtain that response and get his wish.

"Amitabha" means "limitless light." The limitless light is the light of wisdom, the opening of wisdom. Whoever recites well can develop great wisdom and a faultless memory. There's no question about it. "Amitayus" means "limitless life" and "Amitabha" means "limitless light."

The word "Buddha" is also Sanskrit. When I first heard the word "Buddha," it sounded like the Chinese phrase "不大 bu da" which means, "not big." So I explain the term as meaning "not big."

*With neither great nor small,*
*With neither come nor gone,*
*In numberless world systems*
*Buddhas shine light upon each other's*
    *lotus thrones.*

The Buddha is not any bigger than we people are. Rather, he is just the same size. However, he has become enlightened and returned to his inherent wisdom. We are no smaller than the Buddha, and the Buddha is no smaller than we are. But, because our hearts are not pure, because we have not discovered our inherent wisdom or developed great wisdom, we are still common people.

*The Buddha: One who is enlightened.*
*The living being: One who is confused.*
*When enlightened, one is a Buddha.*
*When confused, one is a living being.*

To become enlightened is to become a Buddha. Before enlightenment one is just a living being. When you become enlightened you gain nothing that the living being doesn't have. When confused, one hasn't anything less than the Buddha has. There is no increasing and no decreasing; it's a question of whether you are confused or enlightened. That's where the difference lies.

I will illustrate this with a very simple analogy. Mind you, this is just an analogy. Don't take it literally, because it's all hypothetical. The Buddha is like a university professor – university professors are not Buddhas – you should be clear about that point – and living beings are like students. Every student can become a professor. Every professor can become a student. The Buddha is, however, wiser than professors. He's even higher than a professor! Remember, this is a mere analogy which demonstrates that the Buddha and people are the same.

"Then why should I chant the Buddha's name? Why doesn't the Buddha recite my name?" you wonder. "Why should I recite 'Namo Amitabha Buddha?' Why doesn't Amitabha Buddha recite me, Tim Testu? Why doesn't he recite my name, 'Testu, the Great?'"

That's a good question. In fact, it's got me stumped. I don't know how to answer it, but I'll think up something: Ah! I know! It's because you never made a vow to cause living beings to recite your name. The Buddha Amitabha in the causal ground was a Bhikshu named Dharma Treasury, and he made forty-eight great vows. In every vow he said, "In the future, when my cultivation succeeds and I have become a Buddha, my country will be one of ultimate bliss and purity. The murkiness of the Five Turbidities will not exist in it. All living beings in the ten directions who recite my name will be led to rebirth in my land, where they may realize Buddhahood. As long as one of them has not become a Buddha, I will not accomplish the right enlightenment."

Because of the power of the vows of Amitabha Buddha we have gathered here to recite – with different mouths but with the same sound – "Namo Amitabha Buddha." We are cultivating by relying on the power of the vows of Amitabha Buddha. When we recite the Buddha's name, Amitabha Buddha knows about it. "Hey, I signed a contract with that living being saying that if he kept my name in mind I would teach him to become a Buddha. If I don't guide him to Buddhahood now, the contract is nothing but a lie." And the Buddha hurries right over to guide you to Buddhahood.

Someone says, "But the Western Land of Ultimate Bliss is so far away – hundreds of thousands of millions of Buddhalands – how can I go there? Can I take a plane? How much will the ticket cost? How much is the bus fare? Could I drive myself?"

Don't worry about that. You can arrive in a single thought. You don't have to buy any tickets at all. In a single thought you can be reborn in the Land of Ultimate Bliss. Hundreds of thousands of millions of Buddhalands are not beyond that one single thought.

We now recite "Namo Amitabha Buddha" and there is nothing more important than this work. Don't you see? Last night it was raining and today the sky is clear. In a moment you are all going to make a vow to stop the rain. The rain has got to stop because we are working hard here at our cultivation. I myself don't have the strength, but if you collectively say, "IT IS NOT ALLOWED TO RAIN!..." For these few days while we are cultivating, the least response we can expect is a clear sky. Otherwise, it will be pitch dark at night, and the paths are very muddy. The men don't know this, but the women are really roughing it over there, sleeping in the barn. They have to cross the river, and it is never certain whether they are going to cross the water or whether the water is going to cross them. But I'll tell you:

> *When you're confused,*
> *the teacher takes you across.*
> *When you're enlightened,*
> *you take yourself across.*

When you become enlightened you take yourself across; you carry your own flashlight.

At just this moment Kuo Hang has struck up a false thought. He wants to run into the mountains to live. Isn't that right, Kuo Hang?

Kuo Hang: Yes...

But you have to open your eyes. If you keep your eyes shut, even if you have a flashlight, it will be useless. You'll fall down anyway.

If it doesn't rain, that proves you are all sincere. If it does rain, that will prove that you are not sincere. It has nothing whatever to do with me. It's none of my business. The rain is *your* business.

* * *

(Remarks after the first hour-long evening meditation:)

Since you've been sitting for a long time, if you like you may stretch a bit, but don't get in anyone else's way. You'll notice some people from Gold Mountain are able to enter the sleeping samadhi, because they sleep sitting up every night and so every time they sit down, they nod out. The people who just arrived couldn't do this.

# Everyone can become a Buddha

## Monday, August 18, 1975 (evening)

This afternoon I spoke about Amitabha Buddha, but I did not finish explaining the term "Buddha." I will do so now.

Previously, the Buddha was the same as every other living being. Not only was he the same as human beings, he was the same as all living creatures, even mosquitoes, bees, and ants. Because he shared this kinship he later brought forth the thought of enlightenment. Having brought forth the thought of enlightenment, he practices the Bodhisattva Way, benefiting himself and benefiting others, enlightening himself and enlightening others, helping himself and helping others, saving himself and saving others. There was no selfishness in the things he did; he was open and unselfish. He helped everyone. When he cultivated in the causal ground, he gave up his very life to rescue living beings. The Buddha saw a tiger about to starve to death, and he offered his body to the tiger for food. When he saw a hawk on the brink of death, he fed his own flesh to it, slicing the meat from his bones in order to feed it. Think it over: The tiger is the most ferocious of beasts, but when the Buddha saw that these evil creatures were starving, he gave up his life to save them. Because he had such a great, magnanimous spirit, he became a Buddha.

After he became a Buddha, did he then sit back and enjoy the bliss of Buddhahood? No. He did not forget all living beings. He saved them; he taught and transformed them.

The Buddha has three kinds of enlightenment:

1) Self-enlightenment;

2) The enlightenment of others; and

3) The perfection of enlightenment and conduct.

He enlightens himself and he enlightens all living beings, and he has perfected the practices of his cultivation.

*Perfect in the triple enlightenment,*
*Replete with the myriad virtues,*
*He is called, "Buddha."*

As to the myriad virtues, in every move the Buddha makes, he benefits others, thus perfecting his virtuous conduct. That is why we call him "Buddha." This has been a general explanation of the term.

Not just a Buddha can realize Buddhahood. Everyone can become a Buddha. That is why our faith in the Buddha is not superstition (literally, "confused faith", 迷信 *mi xin*). Buddhism is not like other religions whose leaders claim, "I am the true god. All others are false. No matter how faithfully you believe in me, you will eternally be my inferior. Never can you occupy my position."

Religion such as this is dictatorial, authoritarian, and unjust! On the other hand, everyone can become a Buddha. This is why Buddhism is the most democratic religion, the most just religion. The Buddha is completely devoid of selfishness, thoroughly devoid of desire for self-benefit. He is open, generous, and impartial, straightforward, true, and unprejudiced. He sees all beings as identical with himself and so he wants to take them all across.

Hearing this, someone has become arrogant. Why? It doesn't occur to him that the Buddha became a Buddha by virtue of his cultivation. He says, "Oh, everyone is a Buddha. I don't have to cultivate. I *am* a Buddha! Everybody is a Buddha!"

This person has deviant understanding and heterodox views. It's true that everyone can become a Buddha, but in order to do so, one must cultivate. When you become enlightened you can certify to the result of Buddhahood. If you do not cultivate and have not become enlightened, what kind of a Buddha do you make? You create a stupid Buddha, a confused Buddha. Muddled and dense, you understand nothing. You hear others talk about it, misunderstanding them, yet consider yourself a Buddha, too. But this can't be done because there is no such thing as a stupid and confused Buddha.

Why do I mention all this? Because in the past I have met many people who have held such views and so I decided to tell you about it.

We will now discuss the Pure Land Dharma-door, Buddha Recitation. The Pure Land is the Western Land of Ultimate Bliss, the country of Amitabha Buddha. When the Buddha was in the world, no one understood the Pure Land Dharma-door. That is why not even one of the Buddha's disciples even thought to request instruction in this technique. The Buddha's disciples, with their great wisdom, didn't understand it. No one thought of asking for it, and so the *Amitabha Sutra*, which we just recited, was spoken by the Buddha without request. All the other Sutras which the Buddha spoke were requested by an interlocutor. For example, in the *Vajra Sutra* the interlocutor was Subhuti, who asked the Buddha to speak the Sutra. Since none of the Buddha's disciples understood this Dharma-door of Pure Land recitation – not even the great and wise Shariputra – the Buddha spoke the *Amitabha Sutra* to Shariputra. It is an extremely important Sutra and takes across those of great wisdom. That we now have met to cultivate this method of Buddha Recitation makes Shakyamuni Buddha very happy and pleases Amitabha Buddha a great deal, too.

Simply explained, there are four kinds of Buddha Recitation. The first is "contemplating by thought Buddha Recitation;" the second, "contemplating an image Buddha Recitation;" the third, "holding the name Buddha Recitation;" and the fourth, "real mark Buddha Recitation."

In "contemplation by thought Buddha Recitation" one examines the following verse:

*Amitabha Buddha's body is of golden hue,*
*His fine marks brilliant beyond compare.*
*The white hair-mark winds as high*
*    as five Mount Sumerus,*
*And his purple eyes are deep and clear*
*    as four great seas.*
*Countless transformation Buddhas*
*    appear within the light,*
*With transformation Bodhisattvas—*
*    also limitless.*
*His forty-eight vows*
*    take living beings across*
*In nine grades of lotuses*
*    to ascend the other shore.*

*Amitabha Buddha's body is of golden hue.* Amitabha Buddha's entire body is gold.

*His fine marks brilliant beyond compare.* His characteristics are incomparable. Amitabha's light is unequaled. He has the thirty-two marks and eighty minor characteristics of a Buddha. His brilliant light pervasively illumines all living beings with whom he has an affinity.

Whoever is sincere in his recitation during this session may be illuminated by Amitabha's light. But your heart must be truly sincere. Bring forth your true heart to recite the Buddha's name, and don't fear suffering or pain. You must be extremely sincere and earnest.

*The white hair-mark winds as high as five Mount Sumerus.* In the space between Amitabha Buddha's eyebrows there is a white hair-mark. How big is it? As big as five Mount Sumerus. And how high is Mount Sumeru? Mount Sumeru is the highest mountain there is. None of our mountains are as high.

The empty space that we see is called the Heaven of the Four Kings. Mount Sumeru is twice as high as this heaven. In other words, the Heaven of the Four Kings is located half-way up Mount Sumeru. Amitabha Buddha's white hair-mark is five times as high as Mount Sumeru. How high do you think that is?

*His purple eyes are deep and clear as four great seas.* Amitabha Buddha's eyes alone are as large as four seas. Now, would you say he has big eyes? His purple eyes, bright and clear, are as big as four great seas, so how big would you say his entire body is? His body is as big as one hundred million trichiliocosms.

*Countless transformation Buddhas appear within the light.* Amitabha Buddha emits light from his eyes, his ears, his nose, and his mouth. His entire body pours forth light, and from every hair pore on his body appear Buddhas from boundless universes. See? Your mind can't possibly conceive of anything so big. No one knows how many transformation Buddhas he creates.

*With transformation Bodhisattvas – also limitless.* The Bodhisattvas which appear on every single hair-pore of his body are also boundless.

*His forty-eight vows take living beings across.* He has made forty-eight vows to teach and transform living beings.

*In nine grades of lotuses to ascend the other shore.* His lotuses are divided into nine grades:

1. Superior rebirth in the superior grade;
2. Superior rebirth in the middle grade;
3. Superior rebirth in the lower grade;
4. Middle rebirth in the superior grade;
5. Middle rebirth in the middle grade;
6. Middle rebirth in the lower grade;

7. Lower rebirth in the superior grade;

8. Lower rebirth in the middle grade;

9. Lower rebirth in the lower grade.

Each of these nine grades in turn divides into nine, making nine times nine, or eighty-one grades in all.

Among the eighty-one grades, how big is the largest lotus? It's about as big as one hundred American continents. This should give you a general idea. The bigger your lotus is, the bigger your Dharmabody will be when you realize Buddhahood and sit upon the lotus throne. If your lotus is the size of a single America, then as a Buddha you will also be just about that big. The Buddha's transformation bodies are inconceivable.

This is called "contemplation by thought Buddha Recitation."

As we sit here listening to the lecture, several mosquitoes among us are thinking, "Oh? How can the Buddha be that big? I don't believe it." It's fitting that they don't believe it, because they are so small they can't believe there could be something that big. Not only do they not believe that the Buddha is as big as he is, they also don't believe people are as big as they are. Although they may see a person, they don't know what a person is. They think we are Mount Sumerus. Each one of us is, in fact, a Mount Sumeru. What does that mean? Today I'll reveal this most subtle and wonderful Dharma: Your Mount Sumeru is just your arrogance, your haughtiness, and your disbelief!

Okay. That's all for today. There are still three more types of Buddha Recitation to be discussed. Perhaps someone will tell you in a dream tonight what they are. If not, I'll explain them tomorrow.

* * *

## Incense Chant

*The censer's incense now is lit,*
*    covering the Dharma Realm;*
*The ocean-wide host of Bodhisattvas*
*    inhales it from afar.*
*Most auspicious are the clouds*
*That gather as we now request*
*With hearts sincere and earnest*
*That all Buddhas manifest.*

*Homage to the Enlightened Being*
*Cloud Canopy of Fragrance, Bodhisattva (3x)*

# The Dharma Ending Age

Tuesday, August 19, 1975 (afternoon)

Today is the second day of the Buddha Recitation Session. Yesterday you didn't know what the recitation of "Namo Amitabha Buddha" was all about, and so I explained it to you. By now, each of you should know how to apply effort in reciting the Buddha's name. When reciting, don't sing too loudly or it may injure your energies. However, if you recite too quietly, it's easy to doze off and lose your vitality. When you are napping, you can't recite. If you can't recite, then "Namo Amitabha Buddha" will not be present in your heart. So it is necessary to recite out loud so that your ears hear the sound clearly and distinctly, and your mind contemplates the sound clearly and distinctly. Don't waste even a single second. At all times be mindful of your Buddha Recitation. Say "Namo Amitabha Buddha" with sincerity and concentration.

Your mindfulness should be uninterrupted. Continue reciting at all times without a break. Last night I explained the first of the four techniques of recitation, "contemplating by thought." Today I will continue with the second, "contemplation of an image Buddha Recitation."

When you contemplate using thought, it is not easy to expand the measure of your mind. Amitabha Buddha's Dharmabody is so large that it is difficult to encompass it in thought. You must enlarge the capacity of your mind, and that is not easy to do. As an alternative, you may set up an image of Amitabha Buddha and while facing the image, recite the Buddha's name. Look closely at the white hair-mark between the Buddha's eyebrows. The white hair-mark will emit a great light which will travel to the end of space throughout the Dharma Realm, so that all places receive the illumination. Within Amitabha Buddha's light appear limitless Buddhas and countless Bodhisattvas. This is the method called "contemplation of an image Buddha Recitation."

The third is "holding the name Buddha Recitation" in which one repeats the six-syllable vast name, "Na Mwo E Mi Two Fwo," that is, "Namo Amitabha Buddha." This technique is divided into audible recitation and soundless recitation. Here in the Dharma assembly we practice audible recitation. When the bell is rung everyone recites "Namo Amitabha Buddha" in unison, making a grand, melodious sound. Soundless recitation refers to the period when we sit in silence while single-mindedly reciting "Namo Amitabha Buddha." This is called "silent recitation," or "vajra recitation."

Of all the Dharma-doors in Buddhism, Buddha Recitation is the easiest one to cultivate, as it

*Receives the beings of the*
*three dispositions,*
*And gathers in both the intelligent*
*and the dull.*

Living beings are of three dispositions: a superior disposition, that is, people with wisdom; a mediocre disposition, that is, people of average intelligence; and an inferior disposition, that is, people who are very stupid. This method benefits both the young and the old, and works for both the intelligent and the dull. Intelligent people are those with wisdom and dull people are the stupid ones. People with wisdom who recite the Buddha's name can easily gain a response. People who are stupid who recite will also find it easy to gain a response. Therefore the recitation of "Namo Amitabha Buddha" on the one hand saves effort and on the other costs nothing. It's the most convenient Dharma-door of all. Not only is it convenient, it is the most expedient of all expedient methods, the shortest of all short cuts, the most wonderful of all Dharma-doors. Some people may say, "What's the significance of the phrase 'Na Mwo E Mi Two Fwo?'" Its significance is profound and vast. Its wonder cannot be exhausted in speech, nor can its advantages.

When the Buddha dwelt in the world, that era was called the Orthodox Dharma Age. At that time, the Buddha taught the Dharma and there were genuine Arhats and great Bodhisattvas; the sages were dwelling in the world. The Dharma Image Age followed next, after the Buddha entered Nirvana. During this period people who cultivated the Way were few; those who were attached to external appearances were many. People stressed the creation of Buddha images and many were made, but genuine cultivators were few in number.

After the Dharma Image Age, came the Dharma Ending Age. The Orthodox Dharma Age lasted for one thousand years. The Dharma Image Age lasted another one thousand years. That's two thousand years in all. The Dharma Ending Age endures for ten thousand years. We are now living in the Dharma Ending Age. What does the phrase "Dharma Ending" mean? It means that the Dharma has nearly come to an end and is about to disappear. The "disappearance" of the Buddhadharma involves the disappearance of belief in the Buddha. In the Dharma Ending Age, living beings' faith in the Buddha is not firm. When the Buddha dwelt in the world, people's faith was so firm that if you held a person at knife-point and threatened his life saying, "Don't believe in the Buddha or I'll murder you," he would rather die than surrender his belief. That's how solid in faith the people were during the Orthodox Dharma Age.

In the Dharma Image Age, things were different. If a person believed in the Buddha and someone said, "If you believe in the Buddha, I'll kill you," he'd say "Fine. I won't believe in the

Buddha." People would change their minds because their faith was not firm.

Now, in the Dharma Ending Age, you don't even have to threaten a person with death. You just have to say, "Don't believe in the Buddha," and they quickly reply, "Okay, fine." You don't have to threaten them, just tell them to quit believing and they will. It's very difficult to promote faith. Calculate it for yourself: How many people are there in the world? Among the entire human race, how many people believe in the Buddha? You can lecture the Sutras to these believers every day and they will still waver between doubt and faith. You can conduct a small experiment. Try this. Invite a person out to a movie. He'll accept on the spot and away you go. Then try asking him to a Sutra lecture. He will say, "Ohhh... sitting there for two hours is nothing but suffering and tedium. It's not half as much fun as a movie!" That's the Dharma Ending Age for you. You needn't threaten them with death. You can simply say "If you believe in the Buddha, I'll bow to you three times." And what do you think happens? They snap, "Since you believe in the Buddha, go bow to yourself if you want to bow. Why bow to me?" In the Dharma Ending Age it is difficult to believe in the Buddha. People may believe for a while but then they retreat. They may believe for two and a half days, but before the third day rolls around, they turn back and say, "I'm tired of Buddhism." Tired. See? That's the basic make-up of people in the Dharma Ending Age. Grab somebody by the ear and tell him face-to-face, "Don't talk so much!" and he'll continue to talk, talk, talk too much! That's the way it is. If you tell them not to do something, they insist on doing it. If you tell them to do something, they will insist on not doing it. That's the way beings are in the Dharma Ending Age.

In this age, the Dharma will disappear. The first Sutra to disappear will be the *Shurangama Sutra*. That is why those who study the Buddhadharma should first investigate the *Shurangama Sutra*. As long as someone understands this Sutra the Buddhadharma will not become extinct. As long as there is someone who can recite the Shurangama Mantra, the demon kings, the heavenly demons and those of externalist teachings will not dare come into the world to play their tricks and to make trouble. The Shurangama Mantra is the most miraculous mantra for helping the world. The *Shurangama Sutra* is the primary Sutra which protects and supports the Orthodox Dharma.

The *Shurangama Sutra* will disappear first, and then no one will be able to recite the Shurangama Mantra, because it is too long. For example, many among us have been studying it for over a year and still can't recite it. Basically, the Shurangama Mantra should take six months to learn. The Sanskrit "Shurangama" is transliterated into Chinese as *leng yen*, and those who study it are said to be *leng*, that is, in a daze, for half a year while memorizing it. Here, we have people who have been *leng* for one, two, and even three years, and still have not come out of their "daze."

The *Shurangama Sutra* and the Shurangama Mantra will be the first to disappear. The last Sutra to disappear will be the *Buddha Speaks of Amitabha Sutra.*

When the *Amitabha Sutra* has become extinct, only the six-syllable vast name "Na Mwo E Mi Two Fwo," will remain in the world. It will live another one hundred years and ferry limitless living beings across the sea of suffering. After one hundred years the six-syllable vast name will lose two syllables and only "E Mi Two Fwo" will remain for another hundred years and then they will disappear. At that time people will be undergoing extreme suffering. They will have no blessings at all. Their food will have no nutritive value, even the natural foods. No matter what one eats, it will be harder to swallow than horse manure. Why? Because the people will have no blessings. When the Buddha was in the world the water had more food value in it than our present day milk has. Why does today's water lack nutritive properties? It's because now the people don't have such great blessings.

At that time, people will be as tall as dogs. When their suffering reaches its peak, things will start getting better, and the eon will begin to "wax." We are presently in an eon of "waning." This means that every one hundred years the average lifespan of human beings decreases by one year and their average height by one inch. When it has decreased to the point that an average lifespan is ten years, and an average height is ten inches, about the size of our present-day dogs, people will have sexual desire as soon as they are born and they will also be able to commit murder. That's how rotten they will be. But at that time, the eon will begin to wax, and every hundred years people's lifespans will increase by one year and their height will increase by one inch. When the average lifespan has reached eighty-four thousand years – would you call that a long life? – it will begin to decrease once again. When the average lifespan has waned to eighty thousand years, the next Buddha, the Venerable Maitreya, will appear in the world. Whoever wants to meet him at that time should work hard right now.

We are now conducting a Buddha Recitation Session. We chant "Na Mwo E Mi Two Fwo" from morning till night. It is said,

*Supreme, profound, wondrous Dharma*
*Is hard to meet in a million eons.*
*I see it, accept, hear and uphold it,*
*And I vow to understand the Tathagata's*
    *true principle.*

*Supreme, profound, wondrous Dharma.* It may look to you like Buddha Recitation is very easy, yet this method is quite rare and hard to find. You should all think about it: In America alone, how many people understand the Dharma-door of Buddha Recitation? Many people will say, "Buddhists sit in Zen meditation." Others say, "Cultivate the Secret School. It's fantastic. It's a *secret.*" Very few truly understand how to recite the Buddha's name. In America such a Dharma assembly has simply never been held before. This is the very first time that the deep, deep, and wonderful Dharma has been explained in the countryside. You might say our Dharma assembly is unprecedented in the history of this country. And what is more, people have come from the four directions to attend, including such distant places as San Diego, Los Angeles, and San Francisco. This demonstrates real sincerity. If they were not sincere, they would not have come all this way. They'd be at the movies instead, or out dancing, drinking, playing cards, shooting a few holes of golf, water-skiing, ice-skating, or whatever. However, these people have abandoned such pleasant diversions to chant "Amitabha" in the mountains.

*Is hard to encounter in a million eons.* Although it is hard to meet, you have now encountered it.

*I see it, accept, hear and uphold it.* Now you have met with the Buddhadharma and know how to recite the Buddha's name.

*And I vow to understand the Tathagata's true principle.* Vow to understand the true principles of the Dharma-door of the Pure Land.

You are all sincere and today I am very happy. Why? Because you have evoked a response and stopped the rain. It didn't rain last night and it didn't rain today. That's two days. This proves that you are earnest in your recitation. If it rains tomorrow, you've retreated. But if it doesn't, then you will have created three dry days. If it doesn't rain for a whole week, that will be conclusive evidence of genuine effort on your part.

Since you are all so earnest, I will tell you what I've been doing. In the last few days I have negotiated and signed a contract with the mosquitoes. It says,

> *Mosquitoes are not allowed to bite participants in the recitation session. Should they feel compelled to bite someone, they shall bite me first. This applies equally to all those attending, regardless of whether or not they are my disciples. Mosquitoes are not allowed to make trouble for anyone.*

So they will bite me first because it doesn't matter if the mosquitoes drink a little of my blood; I want to give it away. After this, if anyone is bitten by a mosquito, please report it to me. If bitten by one mosquito, tell me. If two bite you, announce, "I've been bitten twice!" and I'll take it up with them. After all, they did sign a contract and if they don't live up to it, I just might take them to court!

Someone is thinking, "If one does bite me, I won't dare mention it. If I do, Dharma Master, you will say I'm not reciting sincerely." Well, if you don't tell me, you'll just cheat yourself. It's none of my business. Do as you please!

Disciple: Master, just as the subject of mosquitoes came up, one flew by my ear and I believe it is still biting me.

The Master: Oh? Very well, you can take it to Buddhahood. Tell it, "I vow that you will become a Buddha first."

# Cultivation must be done every day

## Tuesday, August 19, 1975 (evening)

The second day of the session has almost passed. I believe it won't rain tonight. That means that during the last two days everyone has been sincere. I don't know if you will continue to be sincere tomorrow. We'll just have to wait and see whether it rains.

While walking and reciting "Na Mwo E Mi Two Fwo," when you hear the large bell, that is the sign that you are to return to your bowing cushions, and the tempo of the recitation is speeded up. I've noticed that many of you are unaware of this. When you recite, keep your hands in front of your chest; this is called the "palms lowered position." Don't let your hands hang down by your belly. They should be right in front of your rib cage, directly below the heart. When you hear the big bell, raise your palms and join them together. Then you no longer recite "Na Mwo E Mi Two Fwo," but just "E Mi Two Fwo." I've noticed a lot of you don't raise your palms at this time, but let your hands hang down or swing at your sides. This is because you don't know about the rules. Although rules are not important, you still have to abide by them. As it is said, "If you don't follow the rules (in Chinese the word for 'rules' is made up of the two words 'compass and T-square') you can't make circles or squares." That is, if you don't follow the rules you won't attain your goal.

Also, when you stand at your places, those who come first should stand up in front and those who follow should stand behind them in the order that they file in. The first to come should not stand in the back so that those who follow have to shove past to find a place. No matter where you go, you should proceed according to the rules for order in the assembly. Then things won't become confused, but will run smoothly. You should all take note of this.

Cultivation must be done every day. You can't cultivate one day and slack off the next. The same applies to following the rules. You have to follow the rules every day. If you don't, you are not acting in accordance with the precepts of the Buddhadharma. So, wherever you go, take care to observe the regulations and don't be sloppy about it.

"Holding the name Buddha Recitation" can be practiced by both the young and old, and those in the prime of life. It is suitable for everyone. Sick people can recite the Buddha's name; healthy people can also recite the Buddha's name. You who are sick suffer from the pains of disease because of karmic obstacles. You should hold the Buddha's name in order to lessen these obstacles. Those who are healthy are perfectly fit to recite the Buddha's name and dedicate their recitation to insure their perpetual good health. Old people who are approaching the end of the road should follow the good path to the end. They should recite the Buddha's name. Young people whose road ahead is filled with limitless light should recite "Na Mwo E Mi Two Fwo," to make the light appear. Thus, the Dharma-door of Buddha Recitation is suitable for every type of person. You can chant while walking, standing, sitting, or reclining. However, when reclining you should not recite aloud. Do it silently. If you recite aloud it is disrespectful. The busiest people can recite the Buddha's name and the most idle people can also recite the Buddha's name.

How do you practice recitation when you are very busy? You practice the "Morning & Evening Dharma of Ten Recitations." In the morning and the evening do "ten recitations." Recite for the length of a single breath, "Na Mwo E Mi Two Fwo," and that is one recitation. Ten such "breaths" is called "ten recitations." In the morning when you get up, wash your face and brush your teeth. Then face the West, or better still, face an image of Amitabha Buddha, join your palms together very respectfully and bow three times. Chant "Na Mwo E Mi Two Fwo" for the length of ten full breaths. Do this in the morning and in the evening. Recite "Na Mwo E Mi Two Fwo, Na Mwo E Mi Two Fwo, Na Mwo E Mi Two Fwo…" until you run out of breath and that counts as "one recitation." Do this ten times in the morning and ten times in the evening. Don't deliberately stretch out the length of your breath or cut it short. It should be very natural. This is called the "Morning & Evening Dharma of Ten Recitations." Do this every day without interruption; it will only take five minutes. Can you recite at other times during the day? Of course you can. The more you recite, the better. With the skill derived from your practice of this Dharma you can be reborn in the Western Land of Ultimate Bliss. This is the most convenient method of Buddha Recitation.

As I said, "Those with wisdom should hold the Buddha's name; stupid people should do it, too." Suppose someone says, "I'm very stupid. Probably it's useless for me to recite." In using this technique, the stupider you are, the better! The wiser you are, the better! No matter how wise you are you cannot exhaust the method of Buddha Recitation. No matter how stupid you are, you are still included within it and it can be your guide.

Among the Buddha's disciples, one in particular was extremely stupid. How stupid was he? When you taught him how to recite "Na Mwo E Mi Two Fwo" – a mere six syllables – he could not remember them. Finally the Buddha thought of a plan.

"Fine," he said, "since you can't remember the Buddha's name, I'll give you two words. Just recite 'sweep clean.'" But he still forgot! He would say "sweep" and forget "clean," and then he would say, "clean… uhh… what was the first word again? Oh! Sweep! Sweep… sweep… Just a minute now; don't tell me, ah… What was the second word?" He'd remember one and forget the other. He was that dumb. None of us here is quite that stupid. Even me. I'm a bit more intelligent than him. Don't you think so? I do. You are all, of course, much more intelligent than I am... Anyway, what was his name? Little Roadside. He got that name because he was born by the side of the road. Although he was very stupid, he later became enlightened when he found out – What did he find out?

He discovered that his mother was a woman! He didn't know that before. The Buddha certified his enlightenment and he gained spiritual powers. See, if such a stupid person can get enlightened, we who are so intelligent will certainly have even more success.

Okay, that's all for today because someone is thinking the idle thought that, "You know, the lectures are really too long."

# The Mosquito Party

## Wednesday, August 20, 1975 (afternoon)

Are there any questions?

Student: I am rather new to Buddhism and would like to know what school or sect you teach.

The Master: What is your name?

Student: Bob.

The Master: Where are you from?

Student: Manhattan.

The Master: At Gold Mountain Monastery we study the entire spectrum of Buddhism. We do not subscribe to any one particular sect or school. We maintain no such divisions.

Student: I recall the Master once saying that we must cultivate our roots where we come from and we must cultivate the Dharma where it comes from. I'm very new and I don't really understand very much, but I do grasp the idea of birth and death. I understand that when things die, new things are born. I would like the Master to expound upon that and tell us more about what the Dharma is and how we can learn to propagate it in the Dharma Ending Age. Like other living things, when the Dharma ends, does it then get reborn?

The Master: Basically, there is no Dharma Ending Age and there is no Orthodox Dharma Age. In fact, the Dharma is a method for cultivating the Way. The Dharma itself is unmoving. People, however, are sometimes diligent and vigorous and at other times they are lax and lazy. After practicing for a time, people often feel that the Dharma is not as fresh and exciting as it was at first and they quit cultivating. When people are vigorous, that's the Orthodox Dharma Age. When people are lazy, it's the Dharma Ending Age. The session we are conducting here is a vigorous one and it is the Orthodox Dharma Age for us. After the session is over, if you don't cultivate and aren't vigorous, it will revert to the Dharma Ending Age.

Another student: Could the Master please tell us more about the third eye?

The Master: There are five eyes, not just three eyes. Where have you heard about three eyes?

Student: Yesterday, when the Master discussed Amitabha Buddha's white hair-mark, I took that to be the third eye.

The Master: That's not the third eye. That's just the white hair-mark. The Buddha doesn't have just three eyes. The Buddha has a hundred thousand, ten thousand, ten million, limitless, boundless eyes. If we living beings cultivate, we too can possess a measureless number of eyes. On every hair pore alone there is an infinite number of eyes. The third eye which non-Buddhist religions talk about is really nothing. They simply have no understanding of what the doctrines of Buddhism are all about. If you cultivate and become a Buddha you will have an uncountable number of eyes and an uncountable number of hands. Gwan Yin Bodhisattva is said to have "a thousand hands and a thousand eyes," but not only has she a thousand eyes, she has more than ten thousand.

Has anyone been bitten by mosquitoes? Certainly a lot of people must have bites?

Student: One.

The Master: That's because you haven't been sincere in your recitation! You haven't brought forth your true heart.

Student: What about the contract?

The Master: The mosquitoes are bound to fail to observe the terms of the contract. There's not the slightest doubt about it. They are just too small to pay attention to things like that. There are too many of them, besides. I can sign a contract with one of them, but another won't keep the agreement, and will close in. They like their independence and are very democratic in spirit. They won't put up with having people supervise them. If I sign a contract with one of them, another will say, "I didn't sign anything! I'm not following any contract," and so they bite.

For example, in this country there are the Democrats and the Republicans. If I signed a contract with one of them, the other would say, "We didn't sign. It's none of our business." Mosquitoes, too, have a lot of different parties and sects.

Mosquitoes have the Mosquito Party. Ants have ant parties and bees have bee parties. Each kind of living creature has its own organizations. Only my Buddhism has no party, no school, and no sect. It is all-inclusive, complete Buddhism. The Buddhism I teach is not Chinese, Japanese, Thai, Burmese, Ceylonese, or Indian. The Buddhism I promote is world-Buddhism, universal Buddhism, the Buddhism of the entire Dharma Realm. The Buddhism I promote I don't even call Buddhism. I call it "the teaching of people." This is because people can become Buddhas. Because all people can become Buddhas, we can call this teaching "the teaching of people." And so, if you are a person, you should believe in Buddhism.

But "the teaching of people" is not an all-inclusive term, so we will give it yet another name, "the teaching of living beings." All living beings are included within it. This includes the living beings who fly in the air, those who walk on the earth, and those who live in the waters, as well as all the plants and trees and all the other types of vegetation. Living beings are born from a union of changing conditions. When the causes and conditions conjoin, living beings are born. So the Buddhism I advocate has been renamed, "the teaching of people," and "the teaching of living beings."

What is more, "the teaching of living beings" has been renamed "the teaching of the mind." Because all living beings have minds, they can all become Buddhas. Thus we call it "the teaching of the mind." The mind, the Buddha, and living beings are three and yet are not different. They are one and the same. That is why I propagate the Buddhism of the entire Dharma Realm and I take it as my doctrine. I am the school of the Dharma Realm and I take it as the body of my teaching. If we looked at it more closely it would look like this:

Name: The Dharma Realm

Substance: The Substance of the Dharma Realm ˙

School: School of the Dharma Realm

Function: The Function of the Dharma Realm

Teaching: The Teaching of the Dharma Realm

So, in name, substance, school, function, and teaching, it is all "the Dharma Realm." It's territory encompasses the entire universe. All living beings live within the Dharma Realm. No matter what religion you follow, you can't go beyond the Dharma Realm. Moreover, there is no way you can deny that you are a living being. All living beings are included within the Dharma Realm. Thus you are encompassed within Buddhism. Whether you are a good person or a bad person, you are included within Buddhism and I consider you a Buddhist whether you consider yourself one or not.

You may say, "But I don't believe in Buddhism." Well, that's your business. You are like a person who ran away from home at an early age and now no longer recognizes his own father. Even face-to-face you no longer know your father. The territory of my Buddhism includes everyone – believers and non-believers alike. Are believers real Buddhists and non-believers not Buddhists? No. Whether you believe or not, I claim you as a Buddhist. The Buddha himself said, "All living beings have the Buddha nature and all can become Buddhas." You can't run away. There's no place to run to! So when my disciples want to draw near, they may do so; if they want to leave, they are free to leave. No matter where you go, I know you'll never run beyond the Dharma Realm. You can't escape the universe, you can't run beyond the Dharma Realm, and that is just my territory. My Buddhism has no limits. If you believe, fine. If you don't, that's even better. If you praise Buddhism, fine. If you slander it, it doesn't matter. I am vigorous whether the situation is favorable or unfavorable. Even if you slander Buddhism, I will still take you across to Buddhahood. For example, yesterday Kuo Li said a mosquito was biting his ear and I told him to make a vow to cross it over to Buddhahood. When you have that kind of vow power, the mosquitoes won't bite you. Another disciple said that a mosquito had bitten him and I told him to take it to jail. He said, "No, no, no..." Even though he was bitten, he wouldn't lock the bug in jail. That's pure compassion.

Even though I said that I had signed a contract with the mosquitoes, some people have been bitten by them. Although a contract was signed, in all matters one should reflect upon oneself, illuminate inwardly. The first doctrine I spoke was the real one. What was that? I said that if you brought forth your true hearts to recite the Buddha's name, no mosquitoes would bite you and no contract would be necessary. If you do not recite sincerely, but strike up idle day-dreams instead, the mosquitoes know what to look for and they'll say, "You! You're supposed to be cultivating and reciting the Buddha's name but all you're doing is day-dreaming. Okay, you can just offer me a bit of your blood. How do you like that?" They can tell just by looking, you know. If your heart is true, then,

> *Better would it be to change the course*
> *of a thousand rivers,*
> *Than to disturb the mind*
> *of a cultivator of the Way.*

The mosquitoes intuit, "That person is busy cultivating and reciting. No matter what, I'm not going to pester him." Although mosquitoes are small, they can tell by looking, and they also know how to distinguish odors. If you have the "Buddha Recitation fragrance," if your heart is true, they won't bite you. If your heart is not true, if you're like me, for example, and do nothing but day-dream… they come to beg from me all the time. The mosquitoes come to ask for a hand-out, and although I'm very stingy, I have to oblige and give them a little blood. The same is true, of course, for all of you as well. You never, ever considered giving away a penny in order to help someone else, so the mosquitoes say, "This guy is a hard case. He's very stingy with his blood and so I'm determined to taste it." They are encouraging you to bring forth the thought of Bodhi, because when they sting and drink a little blood you may wake up a little, "Ah, the Saha world is truly filled with suffering." Because the bite hurts for several days, you can know how bitter samsaric existence is and think, "I must hurry up and recite the Buddha's name and seek rebirth in the Land of Ultimate Bliss where there is no suffering, only happiness. There are no mosquitoes, ants, or other pests there either." And if you do bring forth the thought of enlightenment then the mosquitoes become your Good Knowing Advisors. They truly help you cultivate. You've got to turn the illumination around and reflect inwardly. Ask yourself, "Have I recited in earnest?" That's the important point. Yesterday when I said that I had signed a contract, that was false. What I told you today is the truth.

Someone is thinking, "I came to this recitation session to hear instructional talks; why is he talking about mosquitoes?" Although the mosquitoes are small, they are a topic for a major essay. When we cultivate the Way, we should start from the small, not from the big. One proceeds from the small to the big, from the near to the far, from the lowly to the lofty. So if you can be clear about the things close at hand, you will understand what is going on at a distance.

If you don't want to hear what I have to say, simply forget it. If you can forget it, you're truly mindful of the Buddha. Today I feel sure that you won't forget.

Someone is thinking, "I can forget. When I fall asleep I'll forget it."

That's all too true.

# Ho's Hair Blackener

## Wednesday, August 20, 1975 (evening)

All of you participating in this session should earnestly recite the Buddha's name so that other people will not have to suffer just because of you. If you don't recite sincerely, it will rain, and those who are sincere will be forced to suffer because of you. If the majority of people are sincere, of course it won't rain. There's no question about it. When it rains, the paths are hard to walk, especially at night. It hasn't rained, now, for three days, and that is a great response, but there are still four days left. We'll have to wait and see what happens. Everyone should be mindful; be extremely earnest and sincere as you chant. Don't relax and forget, and don't neglect to join the recitation. You've come from such a long distance, to be careless and flippant at this point would make the experience meaningless. So it doesn't matter who you are, all participants in the Dharma assembly must endure the bitterness and recite the Buddha's name. Be patient, no matter what happens, and continue to recite.

You shouldn't sing too loudly or too softly. When it's time to recite, don't sing like someone asleep and then suddenly wake up and energetically babble to your friends. Don't be like that. You should put all of your energy into reciting the Buddha's name and visualizing Amitabha Buddha. Then you may obtain a response or observe an auspicious sign. For instance, you may see Amitabha Buddha come to rub you atop the crown; he may draw near and cover you with his sash; you may see Amitahba Buddha emitting light. These are all auspicious signs. You may also smell a very strong and fragrant incense, an extraordinary scent, or you may see lotuses. At night you might dream of reciting the Buddha's name or other various portents. If you obtain such a response, it proves that Amitabha Buddha has come to watch over you, to take care of you.

There are other types of favorable signs. Tomorrow, if anyone has experienced such a sign or evoked a response, they can tell me about it. I want to know about it. We've managed to move heaven and earth and stop the rain, so you can expect more portents. No matter who you are, if you see Gwan Yin Bodhisattva or Amitabha Buddha, tell us about it. Anyone can speak up, as long as he tells the truth. Young and old can relate what they've seen and heard because everything we do here is open and democratic. Everything can be known by everyone.

Don't assume that the Dharma-door of Buddha Recitation is a trivial matter. All the Buddhas of the ten directions were born from this practice. At present, Gwan Yin Bodhisattva, Great Strength Bodhisattva, Manjushri Bodhisattva, and Universal Worthy Bodhisattva all continuously recite the Buddha's name. There was once a dhyana master called Yung Ming Shou. He started out as a cultivator of dhyana meditation and later he became enlightened. After his enlightenment he understood that the Dharma-door of Buddha Recitation was the most wonderful and so he began to chant the Buddha's name. Every time he recited "Na Mwo E Mi Two Fwo," a ray of light flashed out of his mouth. What's more, this was no ordinary light. Within the light was a transformation body of Amitabha Buddha! So it is said,

> *One thought of Amitabha,*
> *one thought of the Buddha;*
> *Every thought of Amitabha*
> *every thought is of the Buddha.*

Shakyamuni Buddha taught this Dharma-door without having been requested to do so, because its wonders are manifold, ineffable, and uncountable. The texts say, "Of all the living beings in the Dharma Ending Age, if a billion cultivate, rare will it be for even one to obtain the Way. They shall be taken across only by relying on Buddha Recitation." However, if you recite the Buddha's name, you can end birth and death, and be released from the spinning wheel of rebirth. That is why we call it the most wonderful of Dharma-doors. You shouldn't mistake what is right in front of your eyes. Don't let it slip through your fingers. Don't go to the mountain of jewels and return with empty hands. You see, the recitation session itself is a mountain of jewels. When you come you should at least get a few treasures. What do we consider gems and treasures? There are many kinds of them. Gold is a treasure, silver is a treasure, lapis lazuli is a gem, mother-of-pearl is a gem, red pearls are gems, carnelian is a gem. Ginseng is a treasure! So are *ho shou wu* and *huang ching*. How does ginseng become a treasure? If it weighs nine ounces, it's called a *ren shen* (人參). If it weighs eleven ounces, it's called a "gem." Look carefully, because there's a lot of ginseng in these mountains. Whoever finds a root weighing eleven ounces will live without disasters, without sickness, and have a lifespan as long as that of the gods. As for *ho shou wu* ("Ho's Hair Blackener"), a one thousand year-old piece is considered a gem. Many Westerners have white hair, and the moment they are born they look like old men and women with frosty temples. But there is hope for all of you. Eat a little *ho shou wu* and your hair will turn black and so will your beard. Therefore, we consider it a treasure.

*Huang ching* (Solomon's Seal) was eaten by cultivators who lived deep in the mountains. Because they were far away from civilization and had no way to buy rice or other staples to eat, they subsisted on whatever herbs they could find growing in the mountains. In the *Pen Ts'ao Kang Mu*, a book on Chinese herbs, it says that *huang ching* is a nutritious herb which can prolong your life. It also says that if you eat it, you can fly. The *Pen Ts'ao Pei Yao* (Combining of Herbs) tells of a young woman – like Kuo Fang – who ran away from home after she had been scolded by her stepmother. She ran into the mountains where there was no food for her to eat, no oil, no salt, nothing. She survived by eating *huang ching* and before long she was able to fly through the air. People saw her flying around in space and coaxed her down with some food to eat – a piece of candy? – but once she ate their cooked food, with its oil and salt, she lost her power of flight. Thus, we consider *huang ching* a treasure.

I've heard that the kitchen planned to serve ginseng tea today. Did you drink any? If you did, then when you recite you should have even more energy. You'll have no excuse to doze off. In just a minute we are going to do the Great Transference of Merit Ceremony and you can strike up your spirits and sing so loud that each sound of the Buddha's name pierces the heavens and plows into the earth. I want you to sing so that the gods in the heavens will hear our sound and join in! The creatures in the hells will hear us reciting the Buddha's name and they will bring forth the thought of enlightenment. That will be a great response!

My hair once turned white. I didn't eat any *ho shou wu* but it still turned black again.

# Plant a good seed, reap a good fruit

## Thursday, August 21, 1975 (afternoon)

If anyone has experienced any unusual states, now is the time to tell us about them.

Student: My mind feels a lot clearer than it did before I came here. I feel like when I leave here I will have a few more tools to cultivate the seed that has been planted within me. I've only heard the sounds, "Na Mwo E Mi Two Fwo" a few times, and at first when I chanted it, it didn't mean anything to me. I centered on the concept of putting my trust and faith in "limitless light," and that uplifted me a great deal. I haven't yet seen any tall Buddhas as big as Mount Sumeru with purple eyes, but maybe if I am persistent I will. I'm going to remember this session. I plan to use these tools well.

I have something I would like to share with the people who are planning to take refuge. When I took refuge with the Master last year, I didn't have a clear idea of what I was doing. I was drawn there through faith, very auspiciously, as someone said. Before I left for San Francisco, someone gave me a very meaningful poem which I would like to read:

> *There are ways we travel*
> *Silent, golden and yet unseen*
> *By most who stand behind*
> *The hand of life as it sows the field.*

*Those who know say let it go*
*And it will grow to radiate itself.*
*Never fear,*
*For very near you stands the guardian.*
*The gate he guards is never closed*
*To close inspection.*
*Close your eyes to distracting images.*
*Open your mind's eye and say,*
*   "I am the Buddha;*
*      the Buddha lives in me.*
*   His compassion shines,*
*      and forever lights up my way."*
*There are truths we know,*
*And yet beyond our knowing*
*Still more wait.*
*And again we stand before the guardian*
*Of yet another gate.*

The Master: Does anyone else have anything to say?

Student: Last night I dreamt that I was with my mother, my sister, and three of my cousins and we were all respectfully walking around the Buddha.

Another student: I had some significant visions while I was sitting. I saw a golden sphere with a keyhole in it. A golden key was inserted in it and it began to turn. As it turned, the light intensified. Another vision was that of a formation of jewels. It had a definite pattern and was set in something that looked like highly polished lapis lazuli. The colors were intense reds and golds.

The Master: Who else had an experience? Speak up.

A student: In the world at present there are a great number of people who do not have enough food to eat, who are not properly dressed or housed, while a small minority of people have much more than they can use. I experience a lot of frustration because my actions seem very insignificant and the problems are great. Just what can we do to change these things?

The Master: Worrying about them is of no use. Exhaust your efforts and do what you can and don't ask too much of yourself. An individual has only a limited amount of influence. First rescue yourself, and then you will be in a position to rescue others.

When we stop reciting the Buddha's name and take our seats, at that time you can investigate dhyana or you can continue to recite the Buddha's name silently. It is then very easy to experience a state of "light and peace." What is "light and peace?" It is the beginning sign of entry into samadhi. You may feel as if your body and empty space have united into one. There will be no mark of people, no mark of self, no mark of living beings, and no mark of a lifespan. You are certainly not asleep, but everything has come to a peaceful stop. This is the state of "light and peace." Whoever can stop his idle thoughts can realize genuine wisdom.

This layman just said that many people in the world lack food, clothing, and shelter. Why is this? It's because those who do good are few and those who do evil are many. People who commit many evil acts and do not practice good deeds must undergo this kind of retribution. If you want to alleviate the sufferings of everyone in the world, you must first begin with yourself. How? Do no evil yourself; instead, practice all kinds of good deeds. In this way you can avert the disasters due to afflict us and help the world out a bit. Do as many good deeds as you have the power to do. Exhaust your strength to fulfill your responsibilities, but don't worry too much. If you do nothing all day except sit and think, "People are suffering too much. What can I do?" it is useless. You yourself must do good deeds and cause the world everyday to gain in good and decrease in evil. Then the world will be well, and everyone will have clothing, food, and shelter. It is said,

*Plant a good seed,*
   *reap a good fruit;*
*Plant an evil seed,*
   *reap an evil fruit.*

If you plant ginseng, in the future you will harvest ginseng. If you plant *ho shou wu*, in the future you will harvest *ho shou wu*. You get what you plant. Karma works in the same way fields are planted and harvested.

I have just asked you to speak about your experiences, and I, too, have something to share. This event took place at Gold Mountain Monastery. Once, after a ceremony at which some thirty people took refuge, I asked, "Why did all of you decide to take refuge?" The new disciples had been followers of an outside Way teacher, whom I had given the name, "Shan Lu," "Mountain Deer." When I first came to San Francisco, Shan Lu came everyday to study the Buddhadharma under me. At that time I only lectured on the Dharma once a week, on Sundays. He came every Sunday for two years. Later, a lot of people came to believe in him. During the two years he studied with me, he learned a few doctrines and set himself up as a patriarch, and took disciples. Why did his disciples believe in him? He had money, perhaps as much as a million. Whoever went to him and believed in him had food to eat and a place to live, to say nothing of clothes to wear. Thus they solved their problems of the three necessities. He was seventy or eighty years old, very rich, and very casual. You could eat meat if you liked, drink wine – he would buy you your wine and your meat! – in fact, you could have anything you wanted. There was no moral code at all. They had wine to drink, meat to eat, and they also took drugs, a very progressive pastime back in those days. He failed to teach people even the most basic of the Buddha's precepts and yet he claimed to be an enlightened patriarch. A lot of people, as the word got around, said that he had certified to the fruit of sagehood and others said that he was enlightened. Some really stupid people studied the Buddhadharma with him, while others, the smart ones, thought continually about his money. One day he suffered a fall down the stairs and, without a sign, without a sound, he died. After his death, the group published his books and styled him a patriarch. One night, he appeared to his followers in a dream. He said, "The Dharma I taught you in the past is not ultimate. You should now go take refuge with Dharma Master so-and-so, and study the Buddhadharma with him. That's the right thing to do." So his followers came to me and signed up to take refuge with the Triple Jewel and started studying the Buddhadharma over again.

When you cultivate the Way, it's not easy to meet a genuine good knowing advisor. Some people pretend to be such advisors, and without any real understanding they proceed to teach other people. Shan Lu, for example, was such a one. Later he experienced a twinge of conscience and apologized to his followers. He told them to take refuge with the Triple Jewel and thereby avoid falling into the hells. Of the thirty people who took refuge that day, nearly twenty of them were Shan Lu's disciples. After the ceremony they told me about this dream. They said that Shan Lu had instructed the entire group to come and take refuge. They believed their dream, because over twenty of them had dreamt the exact same dream. They thought it was a miracle. This proves that he wasn't all bad.

So that is a story about an event at Gold Mountain.

# As is the cause, so shall be the result

## Thursday, August 21, 1975 (evening)

In this world, everything proclaims the wonderful Dharma. The mountains proclaim the wonderful Dharma of the mountains. The rivers announce the wonderful Dharma of the rivers. The seas proclaim the wonderful Dharma of the seas. The streams and plains report the wonderful Dharma of the seas and plains. It is said, "Both sentient and insentient things are speaking the Dharma." People speak the dharma of people. Dogs speak the dog-dharma. Cats are speaking the cat-dharma.

For example, cats eat mice. They say that in past lives they liked to kill and in their present life they still like to kill. Tigers are the same way. They proclaim their own wonderful Dharma, and if you understand that they are speaking the Dharma you will not imitate their conduct.

Why are dogs dogs? Dogs are very stingy. They can't give anything away, so they guard the door. When someone comes they bark and bite. Why do they bite? It shows their stinginess. They don't like new people or strangers, so they bite because they are afraid someone will steal the valuables. You could say that they are "wealth-guarding slaves."

There are people who share this attitude towards money. They can't give up a single cent. When you tell them to give, they object violently. Many people keep their money for their sons and daughters. They turn into beasts of burden, scraping together a pittance to leave to their children. A verse says,

*Sons and grandsons have their own blessings.*
*Don't slave like an ox on their behalf.*

Don't be a draft-horse for the sake of your kids. Those who are intelligent will not accumulate money solely for their children. They will give their money away so that in their next lives they can be even wealthier.

You might say, "I don't believe that there are future lives."

Then let's not talk about future lives. Let's talk about tomorrow. Do you believe tomorrow will come? Then, because you can't think in terms of such a distant past, I'll shrink the time period, so that you can understand. Do you believe that yesterday happened? Yesterday was just your former life and today is your present life. Tomorrow will be your future life. If you don't believe in future lives, you still can't deny that there was a yesterday, is a today, and will be a tomorrow. Can you seriously object to this? Yesterday, today, and tomorrow exist and in the same way so do past, present, and future lives. That's a fact.

"Then why don't I know about it?" you ask.

If you knew, you would have become a Buddha long ago. But because you've been muddled and confused through limitless eons until the present, you haven't known your former or your future lives. Thus, you did mixed-up things, like acting as a "wealth-guarding slave," watching the door, afraid that some stranger would come to steal your goods.

When the Buddha was in the world, he once went to a layman's house to accept offerings. In the house there was a dog that stayed under the bed, day and night. He wouldn't allow anyone except members of the family to get near the bed. Anyone else who approached it got bitten. Even the Buddha was not allowed near the bed. The household experimented to see if the dog would bite the

Buddha, and, sure enough, it snapped at him. They asked the Buddha why the dog was so protective of the bed. The Buddha said, "Don't you know? In its last life the dog was your father. Your father spent his whole life earning about three hundred ounces of gold and loved it so much he buried it under the bed. Then suddenly he got sick and died before he could tell you what he had done with it. After his death he hurried right back as a dog to guard the pile of gold. If you don't believe me, start digging and you'll find the gold." They dragged the dog away and did, in fact, uncover exactly three hundred ounces of gold. This proves that stingy people can easily turn into dogs.

Dogs are speaking the dog-dharma. Cats relate the cat-dharma. People expound the people-dharma. In the world, everything speaks the dharma it wants to speak. The important point is whether you understand it or not. If you understand it, the dharma is spoken so you may understand more. If you don't understand it, you're dreaming, and the dharma simply makes you muddled.

Those who have left home proclaim the dharma of those who have left home; those at home expound the dharma of those at home. Bhikshunis speak the dharma of Bhikshunis; Shramanerikas proclaim the dharma of Shramanerikas. Bhikshus speak the dharma of Bhikshus; boys relate the dharma of boys; girls relate the dharma of girls. If you don't understand it, you will become confused. When you understand, you can wake up, become enlightened. This principle extends to the point that Arhats speak the dharma of Arhats; Bodhisattvas speak the dharma of Bodhisattvas. Sound Hearers communicate the Sound Hearer-dharma. Gods speak the dharma of gods, asuras speak the dharma of asuras, and ghosts speak the dharma of ghosts. Animals expound the dharma of animals, hell-beings are moaning the dharma of hell-beings. In the Ten Dharma Realms, each speaks the dharma of its own realm. If you understand that in the Ten Dharma Realms all proclaim their wonderful dharma, you can then become enlightened, you can realize Buddhahood.

Let's talk about people. People with eyes expound a dharma with eyes; people without eyes speak an eyeless dharma. What does this mean? Why do people have eyes? It's because in the past they refrained from doing much evil. Why does someone else lack eyes? Because that person looked down on others. Since he looked down on everyone, he now has no eyes. Why do the deaf expound a deaf dharma? Deaf people in the past liked to mind other people's business. They wanted to hear everything so they listened in on conversations, phone calls, and so forth, and thus they became deaf. Why are mutes mute? Because they indulged in gossip. Before long, they themselves became unable to speak. The deaf, mute, and blind all speak the dharma. Cripples can't walk because they always took wrong roads. They walked down roads they weren't supposed to travel and thus became crippled and unable to walk. Those whose hands are paralyzed got that way because they stole too many things in the past. They are all speaking the wonderful dharma. All of you, when you see something, if you understand it, it's speaking the dharma. If you don't understand it, you're dreaming. Everything is a matter of cause and effect.

To make it even clearer, so that no one will be unhappy, people without legs don't have legs because in the past they danced too much. People without eyes watched dancing, and too many plays and movies. Now, a lot of people are very unhappy with me...

The principle is demonstrated in this verse:

*As is the cause*
  *so shall be the result...*

# Buddhism is just me; I am Buddhism

## Friday, August 22, 1975 (afternoon)

So far, I have explained three techniques of Buddha Recitation: "contemplation by thought," "contemplation of an image," and "holding the name." But I have not yet explained the fourth method which is, "real mark" Buddha Recitation.

The real mark is apart from marks; it is not attached to any distinguishing characteristics. It has left all dharmas behind, and swept away all marks. This is the investigation of the dhyana Dharma-door. Those who truly practice dhyana truly chant the Buddha's name as well. Those who can really recite the Buddha's name are, in fact, investigating dhyana. Dhyana practice and Buddha Recitation both help you to stop your idle thoughts and sweep away your personal desires and random thoughts, so that your original face can appear. This is called real mark recitation.

The Buddha spoke all the Dharma-doors to cure the illnesses of living beings. If living beings had no illnesses, then none of the methods would be of use. But, because we living beings have such problems, the methods are useful. Of the eighty-four thousand Dharma-doors spoken by the Buddha, every Dharma-door is number one. Not one of them is number two. Whichever method is appropriate to your situation, that one is number one. If one is inappropriate, and you can't use it, that doesn't mean that it is not number one, because it may be number one for someone else. So I say that there are eighty-four thousand Dharma-doors and eighty-four thousand of them are number one. Now we are cultivating the method of Buddha Recitation, and some also cultivate the technique of holding mantras. There are various mantras, and there are many different Buddhas, but of all the Buddhas, Amitabha Buddha has the closest affinity with us. We living beings may be likened to iron filings and Amitabha Buddha is like a magnet which draws us in to the Western Land of Ultimate Bliss. The other Buddhas are also like magnets, but their magnetism is not as strong. So living beings should recite the name of Amitabha Buddha and cultivate the Pure Land Dharma-door. This is the first time in the history of America that we have gathered in the mountains to recite the Buddha's name. I believe that we are planting a cause which will in the future certainly produce a grand blossom and bear a great fruit. You can believe this implicitly.

After the session, I will teach you a secret mantra. When you return home, if you want to recite the mantra you may, or if you want to recite the Buddha's name, you may. We'll see who succeeds first in their cultivation. Does anyone have an opinion on this?

Student: Can we still speak about special occurrences? Yesterday during the hour sit, I felt a lot of electrical energy and at one moment I felt very large. My head was in the clouds and a rainy feeling was in the air. Later, I was once more in the clouds only this time I was talking with an entity and I did not want the rain to fall.

The Master: This state may happen to those who cultivate dhyana. I just said that when the session was over I would teach you a mantra and I think now that some people are having a particular idle thought. Someone is thinking, "I'm leaving tomorrow. I might not get a chance to learn it!" Isn't that correct?

Student: Yes.

The Master: Well, if I taught it to you now, would that be okay?

Student: Yes, thank you!

The Master: This is the most wonderful of mantras. Now I will teach it to you audibly, but when you recite it you should do so silently. Don't speak it out loud, because it's a secret mantra, and if you speak it out loud it won't be a secret any longer. Walking, standing, sitting, and reclining, you should always recite this mantra. The mantra's power is very great. For example, if you recite it in the mountains, after five hundred years have passed all the living creatures on the mountain will become Bodhisattvas. Its merit and virtue is that great. If you recite it in the water, after five hundred years all the living creatures in the water will bring forth the thought of Bodhi, and in the future will become Bodhisattvas. Just recite it and five hundred years later all the fleas, nits, and bugs, and all the germs in your own body will also bring forth the thought of enlightenment and become Bodhisattvas. Is this or is this not real power? If you yourself do not wish to become a Bodhisattva, helping other living beings to become Bodhisattvas is a good thing to do. Therefore you can't not recite this mantra. Learn it and recite it!

I will now transmit it to you and you should all pay special attention to it. If you already know the mantra, don't think, "Oh, I know it," and look on it lightly. Those who don't know it should be even more respectful of this dharma.

Now I will teach it to you. Pay attention, because I'm only going to repeat it three times and whether or not you remember it is up to you:

*Om Mani Padme Hum*
*Om Mani Padme Hum*
*Om Mani Padme Hum*

The Chinese pronounce it this way, "Nan, Ma Ni Ba Me Hung," but you can say it either way. It doesn't matter what language you use because the power of the mantra is inconceivable. Take special care to cultivate and uphold this dharma.

* * *

On Friday afternoon, seventeen people took refuge with the Master, including Mr. and Mrs. Brevoort, hosts of the Buddha Recitation Session, and their son, Joshua. At the end of the ceremony, the Master delivered the following short talk to the new disciples:

You should all remember that you took refuge at Buddha Root Farm. I gave young Joshua the Dharma name "Fruit of the Root," (果根 *guo gen*) because he is a Buddha root. All of you who have taken refuge here should be leaders of Buddhism. You must act as models for all peoples. Be good Buddhist disciples and spread Buddhism throughout the entire world, throughout the universe. If there is one person who does not believe in the Buddha, it will be because you have not fulfilled your responsibilities. You should vow to cause all people to take refuge with the Triple Jewel. That will result in great merit and virtue. The *Sutra of Comparative Merit and Virtue* says, "If there were Buddhas in number as the seedlings of rice, stalks of hemp, stalks of bamboo and reeds in the great trichiliocosm, and if you presented those Buddhas with the four kinds of offerings, and then, when those Buddhas passed into extinction, you again made offerings of incense and flowers, food and drink, and built shrines and temples for them, the resulting merit would be great indeed. However, when you yourself take refuge with the Triple Jewel and exhort others to take refuge, the merit from this exceeds the former."

What are the four types of offerings? They are: food and drink, clothing, bedding, and medicine. Although the merit from offerings of flowers and incense and building shrines and temples is considerable, when you encourage one person to take refuge with the Triple Jewel and when you do so yourself, the merit from that action surpasses the merit obtained by making offerings to all those Buddhas. Thus, the result of taking refuge with the Triple Jewel is inconceivable.

Each of you should make Buddhism your own responsibility. Think, "Buddhism is just me; I am Buddhism." Don't set yourself apart from Buddhism. "Not only is Buddhism my religion, but I am going to convert those of other religions to Buddhism. This is my vow."

You should make the Four Vast Vows:

*I vow to save the boundless number of beings.*
*I vow to cut off the endless afflictions.*
*I vow to study the unlimited Dharma-doors.*
*I vow to realize the supreme Buddha Way.*

You should make great vows to spread the Buddhadharma. Okay?

Refuge-takers: Okay!

Of those who took refuge today, many are familiar to me and you need not stand on ceremony. Go ahead and do a good job. Okay?

Refuge-takers: Okay!

# No living being can escape it

## Friday, August 20, 1975 (evening)

Are there any questions?

Student: I would like to know about the coming of Maitreya Buddha. When is he due to appear?

The Master: It's still very early to look for the coming of Maitreya. Those who say that Maitreya is due simply do not understand the situation. Although Maitreya actually comes here all the time, he hasn't yet become a Buddha. When you say, "Maitreya will come," this refers to his return as a Buddha. When will he return? Earlier, I explained the "waxing and waning" principle. That is, every one hundred years our average height decreases by one inch, and our average lifespan by one year. When the average human lifespan, which is now sixty or seventy years, has decreased to ten years, it will begin to increase again. When it reaches eighty-four thousand years, then it will start to decrease. When it has decreased to eighty thousand years, then Maitreya Buddha will appear in the world. So if you calculate the time, it is still in the distant future. Those who are coming now are Maitreya's transformation bodies, not his actual body.

Ultimately, we must go back to the root and return to the source. Everyone can become a Buddha.

A few days ago I said that all the world's religions are included within Buddhism. This is because Buddhism takes the Dharma Realm, the universe, as its substance, and no living being can escape it. Other religions do not teach this. There are Ten Dharma Realms: The Dharma Realm of the Buddhas, that of the Bodhisattvas, the Condition-enlightened Ones, the Sound Hearers, the gods, humans, asuras, animals, ghosts, and the beings in hell. No religion surpasses these Ten Dharma Realms and so all are included within Buddhism; none are not Buddhism. Although they might not admit to being a part of Buddhism, it's only just a matter of time. In the future they will certainly realize this, since there will be no way they can avoid it. They can't run outside of the Dharma Realm. Buddhism takes the Dharma Realm as its substance. I hope that you will all use effort and think about this doctrine.

Many people do not acknowledge that they are Buddhists, but this is no problem. Why not? Because they have not understood that they are within the Dharma Realm. They are like dreamers who are not in control of their actions. They are out of touch with what is really going on. They are also like the insane. Sometimes insane people don't even know that they are human beings. When you ask them what they are, they may answer, "nothing at all," or they may think that they are some strange creature of their own demented fantasy. When a person has lost touch with his humanity you can't rely on his own word when he tries to identify himself. In the same way you can't accept as reasonable the statement that one is not within the Ten Dharma Realms when it is made by someone who does not know the truth.

The *Shurangama Sutra* relates the story of Yajnadatta, the mad man of Shravasti, who one day looked in the mirror and noticed that the person reflected in it had a head. At that point, he lost his reason and said, "How come that person has a head and I don't? Where has my head gone?" He then ran wildly through the streets asking everyone he met, "Have you seen my head? Where has it gone?" He accosted everyone he met, yet no one knew what he was doing. "He already has a head," they said. "What's he looking for another one for?"

There are a lot of people just like poor Yajnadatta.

Are there any more questions?

Student: Are there people who have written about Buddhism, other than yourselves, who are worth reading? Most writers come from a Western orientation and this tends to lead them to alter the doctrines.

The Master: There are other translations, but it is not a question of relative worth. Many previous translators of Buddhists texts were priests, ministers, scholars or professional writers. Although they did translate Sutras, they didn't necessarily understand the Buddhadharma. However, their translations cannot be said to be of no worth – they sell; people buy them. Thus they are worth something. But their principles do differ from the orthodox tradition. The translations done at Gold Mountain Monastery are done by Bhikshus, Bhikshunis, Shramaneras, Shramanerikas, laymen and laywomen, professors, and scholars of the Buddhadharma who all work together. They translate Sutras from within the Buddhadharma. Previous translations were largely done by people standing outside of Buddhist study, training, and practice. Even if these Sutras were translated by Buddhists, they represent only one person's opinion. They were never subjected to the scrutiny of others, never criticized by anyone and inaccuracies passed unchecked into print. It is not, then, a question of worth; it's a question of validity. Previous translations do exist, but the difference is here: The translators have an external viewpoint – they do not stand inside the study and practice of the Dharma. "Outsiders" don't have a genuine, reliable understanding. That's where the problem lies.

The translations done at Gold Mountain Monastery are checked and criticized by several committees of trained, practicing Buddhists. We do not claim that our translations are perfect, but we do strive for perfection. We don't substitute Christian terminology for Buddhist technical terms, so that nothing substantially Buddhist remains in them. Many of the older translations done by clergymen or scholars became vehicles used to talk about the doctrines of

Christianity. We have been investigating the Buddhadharma for many years yet there are many things we do not understand. How much the less can those who have never looked into Buddhism be expected to render the original meaning of the Buddhist Sutras?

We would not dare to say that our translations alone have worth. We would simply not say that. But we are trying to do a good job; we are striving for perfection.

Whenever you go to a Buddhist temple you should be humble. Do not be arrogant. You should feel that everyone else is better than you, and that you have much to learn from them. For example, when you bow to the Buddha, don't stand in the center aisle, because that is the space reserved for the Abbot. Bow to one side. Don't cause those who see you to think, "Oh, your teacher is really stupid. He hasn't taught you anything. You don't even know how to bow to the Buddha."

# People seek out their own kind

## Saturday, August 23, 1975 (afternoon)

Questions?

Student: Yes. When Gwan Yin Bodhisattva succeeds Amitabha Buddha in the Land of Ultimate Bliss, where will Amitabha Buddha go?

The Master: He's going to go right into your heart.

Student: When you are born in the Land of Ultimate Bliss, do you stay there until you are a Buddha or get enlightened, or do you stay only briefly and then leave?

The Master: You become a Buddha right there. Those born in the superior grade of the superior lotuses become Buddhas as soon as they appear. Those born in the lower grade of the lower lotuses must wait ninety great eons to become Buddhas.

In the Land of Ultimate Bliss there are thirty-six billion, one hundred nineteen thousand, five hundred Buddhas all called the "Guiding Master, Amitabha Buddha." Yesterday, I said that Amitabha Buddha was like a magnet and that all living beings are like iron filings. When iron filings meet a magnet they are irresistibly drawn to it. I also said that the other Buddhas were like magnets, but their magnetism was not as strong as Amitabha's. Several people couldn't sleep last night because they were having this false thought: "If all the Buddhas are like magnets, how come some of them have a stronger magnetic field than others? How can their powers be different?" Today, when I asked if there were any questions, no one dared bring the matter up, but I will answer it anyway. It is because Amitabha Buddha has made forty-eight vows, and these vows are like the power of a magnet. Other Buddhas have also realized Buddhahood, but they have not made these forty-eight vows and so their power is not as great. Thus, in cultivating the Way, one must make vows. If there are vows, success is certain. Vows are like a lamp that illumines the road ahead. When you are walking, if you have a lamp to light the path, it is very easy to travel. Each one of us should make vows. At Gold Mountain Monastery, every year on the eighth day of the twelfth lunar month, the anniversary of the enlightenment of Shakyamuni Buddha, those who wish to do so may make vows. That day is called "vow day." Although the word vow (願 *yuan*) in Chinese sounds the same as the word for resentment (怨 *yuan*), it is not a day of resentment. Some people resent heaven and curse their fellow human beings saying, "Heaven! You really don't know how to do your job. You are so unjust! And every soul on this Earth is wrong!" People like that think everybody else is in the wrong.

Can one make vows at other times as well? Yes. However, that particular day is the anniversary of Shakyamuni Buddha's enlightenment and so, when we make vows on that day, he is very pleased. "Oh! In the world another living being has made vows because of my enlightenment. Good indeed! Good indeed! Good man, good woman, it is good indeed that you have made such vows. I shall certainly help you fulfill them."

Yesterday, I taught you the mantra Om Mani Padme Hum, and some people had these idle thoughts, "Perhaps I was one of the bugs on a Dharma Master's body five hundred years ago. Since he recited the mantra, I've now become a human being and taken refuge with the Triple Jewel. Probably that's what happened." That's their false thought. Well, I'm not going to answer that question. Maybe Little Kuo Fang was such a bug. She likes to eat candy and when I recited the mantra it probably kept turning things into candy...

Today, I will continue speaking about Amitabha Buddha. It's not the case that there's just one Buddha, or two Buddhas. In fact, there are as many Buddhas as there are grains of sand in the River Ganges, and they dwell in the ten directions. What are the ten directions? They are: North, east, south, west, north-east, north-west, south-east, south-west – that's eight directions. Then add the zenith and the nadir and you have ten directions. In each of the ten directions there are Buddhas in number like the sands in the Ganges. The Buddha is a living being who has become enlightened. As many living beings as there are, there are that many Buddhas. Can you count the number of living beings that currently exist? There's no way to count them. You can't even reckon the exact number of human beings. There's no way to count them, no matter what scientific methods you use, including computers! Even if you could count the human population, could you count the mosquitoes? How many are there in the whole world? You can't count the mosquitoes, you can't count the ants, you can't count the bees… all the insects, and the birds, all the living creatures. And the Buddhas are also like that. There are so many you could never count them. For every living being, there is a Buddha, and that Buddha will take that living being across. Thus, we talk about the Buddhas of the three periods of time throughout the ten directions. The three periods of time are: the past, the present, and the future. A few days ago I mentioned that some people do not believe in past, present, and future lives, especially rich people. They don't believe at all in future lives. They just enjoy themselves, do business, and pile up a fortune thinking that they are "getting the most out of life." They make it their life's work to live to the hilt. If they want to drink, they drink; if they want to eat meat, they eat meat; if they want to run around, they run around, and they think it's a good deal, that they are living "the good life." But they are wrong.

*Why is one wealthy in one's present life?*
*It's because in the past one gave to the*
*    Sangha and aided the poor.*
*Why is one poor in one's present life?*
*It's because in the past one refused*
*    to practice giving.*

In past lives, when you had money, you didn't give, and so now you are poor. You were afraid if you gave away your money that you wouldn't have any for yourself. "I'll be stone broke. Why should I give my money away? That's too stupid." You held on to every single cent, squeezing it so tightly that it turned to water in your hand. Those so terribly afraid of being poor, in their next life are, in fact, poor.

*Why is one handsome in one's present life?*
*It's because in the past one offered*
*    incense, flowers, and lamps to the Buddha.*

Suppose a person is extremely attractive. Everyone who meets him respects him and is fond of him. In general, no one dislikes him. Why is this? It's because that person made offerings of incense and flowers, and lit lamps before the Buddhas in past lives.

Everything is a matter of cause and effect. So it doesn't matter whether in your past lives you were an Indian, Chinese, Burmese, or Thai – at sometime or another you changed your residence. You may live in one "house" for a while, but eventually you will have to pack up and move. The principle of cause and effect works in human life in the same way. There's nothing strange about it at all. In the world:

*The good walk together, and*
*The evil run in packs;*
*People seek out their own kind.*

Buddhists associate with Buddhists. Those who believe in ghosts gather with those who believe in ghosts. Those who have faith in demons stay with those who have faith in demons. Students associate with students. Politicians associate with politicians, businessmen with businessmen, laborers with laborers, ginseng growers with ginseng growers.

What brought this group together? We are all investigating the Buddhadharma, and we did so in former lives. In former lives we made vows to propagate the Buddhadharma, and in this life, quite unwittingly, we have gone down that road again. This is because we vowed to spread the Dharma in past lives. Here in this country where there is no Buddhadharma, because of past vows, we have come to plant the Buddhadharma. In past lives we made such vows and in the present we are carrying them out. So don't ask what nationality you were in a former life or how you got reborn in America. No matter who you were in your last life, you were a person. So you don't need to ask. Right?

No matter what nationality people are, they should be good towards everyone. They should think, "If someone is bad to me, I will forgive them. I will treat everyone well. I will forget the evil done to me and remember only the good. I will look for the good points in others and not for their faults." If everyone were like that, there would be no war in the world. Why are there wars? It's because everyone looks for the faults in others, and no one looks for the good points. So, day by day, there is more and more hostility in the world.

# Making revolution in the Sangha

## Saturday, August 23, 1975 (evening)

Does anyone have anything to say?

Student: The Master has likened the experience of enlightenment to earning a college degree, that is, you work for years and years until suddenly at graduation you receive your diploma. Shakyamuni Buddha had to cultivate for three great eons and for another one hundred eons before he perfected his fine characteristics. Finally, he became a Buddha. Is the "schedule" for enlightenment fixed in any way or could one, through diligent cultivation, exhaust one's karmic obstacles in a single lifetime and obtain the Buddha's wisdom very quickly?

The Master: Have you heard the story of Dhyana Master Miracle on the High Peak? You can find the answer there. The story goes like this:

The Miracle on the High Peak...

Dhyana Master Kao Feng Miao always fell asleep during his meditations and so to prevent this he went to sit on top of a mountain. He sat atop a rock which looked like an inverted lotus, and the drop was who knows how long. He knew that if he fell asleep he would fall over the edge and be smashed to a pulp. The first day he sat very well. The second day went fine. But on the third day he dozed off and slipped over the edge. "I'm finished!" he thought, but just then Wei T'o Bodhisattva reached out his hand and snatched him out of the air.

Kao Feng Miao thought, "Wei T'o Bodhisattva is protecting me. How many cultivators are there like me in the world?"

"There are as many as the hairs on a cow," answered Wei T'o, "and since you are so arrogant, I won't protect your Dharma for the next eighty thousand eons."

Hearing this, Kao Feng Miao was deeply ashamed. He repented greatly. He cried and cried until he even forgot about sleeping. He cried himself into a stupor, forgetting everything, until suddenly, as if waking from a dream, he realized, "Before I knew that Wei T'o was protecting my Dharma, I cultivated the Way. Now, I will continue to cultivate whether he protects me or not." And he sat down again, more determined than ever. It wasn't long, however, before he fell asleep again and fell over the edge. Oddly enough, the same hand reached out and caught him.

"Who's that protecting my Dharma?" he asked.

"It's me, Wei T'o Bodhisattva," came the reply.

"Hey, Old Wei," said Kao Feng Miao, "You don't keep the precepts either. You told a lie!"

"I did not," countered Wei T'o.

"You said you wouldn't protect my Dharma for eighty thousand eons and here you are protecting my Dharma," challenged Kao Feng Miao.

Wei T'o replied, "Because of your one thought of genuine repentance, you overstepped eighty thousand great eons of retribution and so I came to save you."

The important point was that in his one thought of repentance he was able to cancel out, to pass beyond, as it were, eighty thousand eons. That should answer your question. If the "schedule" for enlightenment was fixed, it would turn into a dead dharma, not a live dharma. It would be a fixed dharma, and there simply are no fixed dharmas. Shakyamuni Buddha cultivated for three great eons, but that's just a manner of speaking. Three great eons don't go beyond a single thought; one thought is just three great eons. Haven't you been listening to the *Avatamsaka Sutra*? Do you know how many great eons you have already cultivated? Maybe you have been cultivating for six great eons.

Student: Perhaps not.

The Master: How do you know that five hundred years ago you weren't a flea on the body of a Dharma Master who recited Om Mani Padme Hum?

Student: Perhaps I still am.

Another student: The Gold Mountain Doctrine in two separate places says that "we do not change," and it also contains the phrase "make revolution in the Sangha." I was wondering, since you are the Orthodox Dharma, how can you advocate revolution?

The Master: The phrase "making revolution in the Sangha" is not part of the doctrine itself. The first three statements are the Gold Mountain Doctrine: "Freezing we do not scheme. Starving, we do not beg. Dying of poverty, we ask for nothing." What follows is the transmitting of the Buddha's mind-seal in accord with true principle.

And as for revolution, it is just because we are the Orthodox Dharma that we need a revolution. Every place else, it's the Dharma Ending Age. If you don't shake up the Dharma Ending Age, you're neglecting your responsibility. Revolution refers to revolution in the Dharma Ending Age, not in the Orthodox Dharma. You don't realize how things are done in Asian Buddhism. For example, during the Incense Praise, the Abbot lights the first stick of incense and when he is done he signals to the lay people to offer incense. The one who wants to light the first stick has to pay $5,000 or $50,000 and only then can he approach the altar. We don't do it that way here. No one pays to light incense. In Asia, the first person to light incense pays $5000, the second, $4000, and the third,

$3000, and so on. In their eyes, the one who gives the most money is the greatest Dharma protector. Do you think this is right?

At Gold Mountain Monastery the poor and the rich bow to the Buddha on equal ground. There is no discrimination made. It's not the case that if you give more money, you're number one. In China, monks recite Sutras for people, to help the dead, and for this service one pays $10,000 or maybe $100,000. In general, "the more money, the better." Money is regarded as all-important, and other things, the Sutras, the Dharma, the Buddha, and the Sangha, are not held in such high esteem. So it is with Asian Buddhism. If you bow to the Buddha, you have to give money. Otherwise the Buddha won't notice you. If you give more money the Buddha's eyes may open wider. So it is in the Dharma Ending Age.

Things are different in America. Here, it's not the case that the one who gives the most money is first and the one who gives only a little must stand behind. We don't do things that way. It's not that we don't accept money, rather we don't place such great importance on it. This kind of an attitude is revolutionary! This is "revolution in the Sangha." We are making revolution against the improper elements, the elements that bring the advent of the Dharma Ending Age. Thus, we uphold the Orthodox Dharma by purging it of its "unorthodox" elements.

The following sentences say, "We accord with conditions, but do not change." This means that we follow the conditions, but do not stray from our basic doctrines. We don't go around criticizing others and in this way we "accord with conditions." If other people do things differently, we don't hinder them.

However, we never change in our basic principles. We insist on doing things correctly ourselves and that's what is meant by "we do not change, but accord with conditions."

The "revolution" means that all the improper customs and habits must be eliminated. We want to do away with the Dharma Ending Age and usher in the Orthodox Dharma.

That was a good question. How can the Orthodox Dharma conduct a revolution?

This afternoon we spoke about all the Buddhas in the Dharma Realm. It is said,

> *Of the Buddhas of the three periods of time*
> *throughout the ten directions,*
> *Amitabha Buddha is foremost.*

Amitabha Buddha is number one. This is because of the power of his vows. This power is so great that when you recite "Na Mwo E Mi Two Fwo," you can very quickly realize Buddhahood. To become a Buddha, all you need to do is recite the Buddha's name. The Dharma-door of Buddha Recitation works on the same principle as the mother-son relationship. Those who recite the Buddha's name are like the "sons" and the Buddha is like everyone's "mother." Whoever recites Amitabha Buddha's name is like Amitabha Buddha's son. In the *Shurangama Sutra*, in the section in which the twenty-five sages explain their ways to enlightenment, the Bodhisattva Great Strength says, "It is like a mother thinking of her son. If the son has gone to roam..." If the son leaves his mother, it is hard for his mother to find him again. But if the son wants to find his mother, all he has to do is return home. If the mother thinks of her son, but the son cares not for his mother, he will run farther and farther away. If the mother thinks of her son and the son is mindful of his mother, then they will always be together. Everyone of us are the sons and daughters of Amitabha Buddha. All we need to do is wish to return home and we can. If we don't want to return home, our father and mother might wait for us, but there is nothing they can do. So it says, "Amitabha Buddha is foremost."

> *In nine grades,*
> *he saves living beings.*

There are nine grades of lotuses, each of which has nine grades, making eighty-one grades in all. Whoever recites Amitabha Buddha's name causes a lotus flower to bloom in the pools of the seven jewels in the Land of Ultimate Bliss. The more you recite, the larger your lotus blossom grows. If you recite just a little, your lotus will be small. If your lotus is big, you will rapidly become a Buddha. If your lotus is small, it will take a little longer. If you don't recite, your lotus will wither and die. If you want your lotus-grade to be a high one, you should recite more. Recite sincerely. If you don't care whether or not you get a low grade, then you can be lazy and not recite – but your lotus will vanish.

*His awesome virtue is unfathomable.*

The power of Amitabha's great awesome virtue is incomparable. No other Buddha can compare with him.

Would anyone like to ask a question?

Student: Sometimes children have invisible playmates. I was wondering what they really are. I had a friend whose child played with a whole bunch of them, but when he misbehaved, he blamed the invisible playmates for his mistakes, and they all disappeared.

The Master: Who knew about this?

Student: His mother.

The Master: Could she see them?

Student: No, but he played with them for hours and hours.

The Master: They may have been ghosts or immortals. Children wouldn't recognize them as ghosts or immortals and might treat them as playmates. Some children can see such beings. When children cultivate the Way, they can very easily succeed. I've often said that for boys under the age of sixteen and girls not yet fourteen, it is very easy to become enlightened, provided they work hard at their cultivation and meet with a genuine Good Knowing Advisor. It's easy for them to accomplish the fruits of the Way. This is because they don't discriminate all the true/true – false/false things going on in the world. They don't deal with all those "you cheat me and I cheat you" affairs that go on. As soon as they go to school and learn how to use a "cheat-sheet" then it's no longer as easy for them to realize the Way.

# The Five Precepts

Sunday, August 24, 1975 (afternoon)

Questions?

Student: I was wondering if living beings come into existence at a given point in time or if their existence is beginningless. If the latter is the case, then is there a fixed number of living beings? If they do have a beginning, an origin, what is it?

The Master: Their origin is the cipher: **O**. As for the Zero, where does it begin and where does it end? That's the "beginningless and the endless." When you break open the cipher: **O**, it becomes the number one: —. In English it stands up on end like this: **1**. When this happens there is a beginning.

When there is the One, then "two" comes into being. With two, comes three, with three comes four, five, six, seven, eight, nine, ten, and on up to infinity. So how many living beings are there?

Another student: If you twist the Zero, it turns into the sign for infinity: ∞.

The Master: That's just the *yin-yang* symbol: ☯. Westerners just draw it differently.

In cultivating the Way you must cultivate to attain the One, and then turn the one back into the Zero. That's called "returning to the root and going back to the source." Does that answer your question?

Student: Yes. It's a question of cultivating the Way.

The Master: When you cultivate, you cultivate the One to return to the Zero. Everyone has forgotten about the One, to say nothing of the Zero. They don't even know what the One is all about.

> *When the heaven obtains the One, it's clear;*
> *When the earth obtains the One, it's serene.*
> *When people obtain the One, they become sages.*

When heaven obtains the One, the sky is clear. For ten thousand miles there's not a cloud. When the earth obtains the One, there are no earthquakes. People who obtain the One are sages. If you can then cultivate the One, turn it into a Zero – that's just the Buddha.

Any other questions?

Student: Could the Master please explain the five precepts?

The Master: As to the five precepts, they prohibit killing, stealing, sexual misconduct, lying, and taking intoxicants. Why should one keep the five precepts? In order to:

> *Do no evil, but*
> *reverently practice good deeds.*

Do not kill; do not steal; do not commit sexual misconduct; do not engage in false speech; do not take intoxicants. If you observe the five precepts, you do not do these five kinds of evil deeds and you instead practice good acts.

Why should one refrain from killing? It is because all living beings have a life; they love their life and they do not wish to die. Even one of the smallest creatures, the mosquito, when it approaches to bite you will fly away if you make the slightest motion. Why does it fly away? Because it fears death. It figures that if it drinks your blood you will take its life. From this you can see that all living beings love life and do not wish to die. Especially people. Everyone wants to live and no one wants to die. Although people sometimes commit suicide, ordinarily people do not seek death. Suicide is a special exception to the principle. That is why we should nurture compassionate thoughts. Since we wish to live, we should not kill any other living beings. That explains the precept against killing.

Stealing: If you don't steal, in the future no one will steal from you. A lot of you have heard this verse I wrote:

*If in this life you don't cage birds,*
  *in future lives you will not sit in jail.*
*If in this life you do not fish,*
  *in future lives you will not beg for food.*
*If in this life you do not kill,*
  *in future lives you'll suffer no disasters.*
*If in this life you do not steal,*
  *in future lives you won't be robbed.*
*If in this life you commit no sexual misconduct,*
  *in future lives you will not be divorced.*
*If in this life you do not lie,*
  *in future lives you will not be deceived.*
*If in this life you do not take intoxicants,*
  *in future lives you will not go insane.*

This covers the general meaning of the five precepts.

Some people say, "Of the five precepts, the four which prohibit killing, stealing, sexual misconduct, and lying are very important. But taking intoxicants is a very commonplace thing. Why prohibit that?" When you consume intoxicants, it becomes very easy to break the other precepts. Thus, we ban such things as drinking alcohol, smoking tobacco, and taking any kind of intoxicating drugs.

Some people say, "The five precepts don't specifically prohibit smoking tobacco or taking drugs. Doing those things is not in violation of the precepts." These people are wrong. The precept against intoxicants also prohibits smoking tobacco, taking drugs, and using all intoxicating substances – including marijuana and opium.

Once there was a layman who received the five precepts. At first they were very important to him and he strictly observed them. After a time, his old bad habits surfaced and he longed for a taste of wine. He thought, "Among the five precepts, the one against drinking is really unnecessary. What's wrong with a little glass of wine?" He bought three pints of brandy and downed them. As he was drinking, the neighbor's little chicken ran into his house. "They've sent me a snack!" he thought. "I'll put this chicken on the menu to help send down my brandy." He then grabbed the bird and killed it. This is a distinctly Chinese story and not a Western story. Why? Chinese people like to eat hors d'oeuvres with their alcohol. Westerners don't need snacks to send off their wine. So, this layman couldn't possibly have been a Westerner. Anyway, because he drank the wine, he wanted the meat and thus broke the precept against killing. Since he took the chicken without the owner's permission, he also broke the precept against stealing. Then the neighbor lady walked in and said, "Say, did you see my chicken?"

Drunk as he was, and full of chicken, he slurred, "No… I didn't see no chicken. Your old pu… pu… pullet didn't run over here." So saying, he broke the precept against lying. Then he took a look at the woman – she was quite pretty – and forthwith he broke the precept against sexual misconduct. A little drink of brandy led him to transgress all five of the precepts. Therefore, the precept against taking intoxicants is also very important.

You may be wondering, "You have said that to keep the precepts is to do no evil and to practice all good deeds, but I wonder if this is really the case?"

If you have your doubts, then of course there will be problems. But if you have no doubts, your good roots will certainly deepen and grow stronger. What is more, when you uphold each precept, five good spirits come to support you and protect you. That makes twenty-five Dharma protecting spirits looking out for you if you keep the five precepts. If you keep them well, you can turn disasters into lucky occurrences and transform difficulties into auspicious events. You will encounter no tragedies or calamities. Those are the advantages of keeping the precepts.

Last night we talked about Amitabha Buddha, and today we shall continue. Everyone has now taken refuge with Amitabha Buddha; we are now Amitabha Buddha's disciples. We should be greatly ashamed of our past conduct and repent of the offenses we have committed through the three types of karma.

What are the three types of karma?

The karma created through the body, of which there are three types. The karma created through the mouth, of which there are four types. The karma created through the mind, of which there are three types.

The mind creates three kinds of evil karma: Greed, hatred, and stupidity. Greed: You might say that greed is just insatiable desire. Then, if you fail to obtain the object of your desire, you grow hateful. Once you are hateful, you become stupid. You then pay no attention to heaven and earth; you heed nothing and no one, and you do things which are upside-down.

There are four evils committed with the mouth. The first is irresponsible speech, speech in which deviant knowledge and views are expressed, rather than proper knowledge and views. The second is false speech, that is, lying. The third is abusive speech, that is, scolding people. Double-tongued speech involves talking about the faults of one person to another person, and then relating the second person's faults to the first party. "Do you know what Lee said about you?" he says to John, and then to Lee he says, "Do you know what insulting things John has been saying about you?" This is like the question yesterday about the invisible playmates. She said they disappeared as soon as the child started to slander them. If invisible friends disappeared as soon as the child started to slander them, you can bet that the visible ones would be even more upset.

Now "double-tongued" definitely doesn't mean that in one mouth you have grown two tongues. It means that you speak in two different ways. You cause dissention and generally create trouble.

The three types of evil committed by the body are killing, stealing, and sexual misconduct. All these kinds of bad karma together form the ten evils. Not committing the ten evils is called practicing the ten good acts.

Students of the Buddhadharma, stop doing the ten evils! Always practice the ten good acts!

The ten evils and the ten good acts are created through the three karmas of body, mouth, and mind. When the three karmas are pure, you will not commit the three types of bad karma. We who recite the Buddha's name should make vows together to obtain a response at all times. Then, when we approach the end of our lives, all the various qualities of the Land of Ultimate Bliss will appear before our eyes. So those who participate in Buddha Recitation should cultivate hard so that we may all be born in the Land of Ultimate Bliss. When you recite the Buddha's name keep these thoughts in mind. Who's got a question?

Student: As to the precept against taking life in relation to not eating meat, I want to ask how we can live without taking life. Plants, for example, seem to have a higher consciousness than most animals. They have a consciousness that's everywhere at once. They display emotions and recognize individuals. Personally I don't feel any more comfortable eating plants than I do eating animals. According to scientific experiments, you can pinch one plant here and its partner will feel the pain at exactly the same time even though it is a thousand miles away. Since they have emotions, how can we kill and eat them any more easily than we can kill and eat animals? How can we stay alive in this world?

The Master: That which has a life is said to be "sentient." Plants are said to be "insentient." This includes the earth, wood, rocks, and minerals. Rocks may appear to be insentient, but they are alive. Their "life" is a bit less, however; it's not as complete, and cannot be compared with that of human beings. Human beings have eight consciousnesses and emotional feelings as well. Although we can say that plants have emotional feelings, they are incomplete. They are called "senseless rocks."

In China, Dharma Master Tao Sheng lectured on the *Nirvana Sutra*. The first half of the *Nirvana Sutra* said that *icchantikas*, that is, unbelievers, did not have the Buddha nature. Dharma Master Tao Sheng said, "Icchantikas also have the Buddha nature." When he said that, all the other Dharma Masters objected. "The Sutra plainly says that icchantikas don't have the Buddha nature, how can you say that they do?" and they told everyone to avoid his lectures. So Dharma Master Tao Sheng went up to Hu Ch'iu Mountain and lectured to the rocks. He addressed them saying, "I say that icchantikas have the Buddha nature. What do you say?" At that point the rocks nodded their heads! It is said,

> *When Sheng, the Venerable,*
> *spoke the Dharma,*
> *Even the rocks*
> *nodded their heads.*

This proves that insentient things also have the Buddha nature.

Student: Well, then, how *does* one justify taking life in order to remain alive in this world?

The Master: If you were to be very strict in your interpretation, then even eating vegetarian food is killing. But it's a bit less serious. If you did not eat, you could not stay alive. "Killing" vegetables is less offensive to one's compassionate sensibilities than wantonly killing animals for food. Killing animals creates thoughts of hatred, not of compassion. Your compassion grows lighter while your hatred increases.

Since plants have no blood or breath how can we prove that they have "life?" Ginseng, for example, after 1500 years can turn into a human being. It can transform into a child and run around. These transformations are called "spirit immortals."

Student: Yes, but if you look at it another way, when you eat one bowl of rice, you take the life of all the grains of rice, whereas eating meat you take only one animal's life.

The Master: On the body of one single animal are a hundred thousand, in fact several million little organisms. These organisms are fragments of what was once an animal. The soul of a human being at death may split up to become many animals. One person can become about ten animals. That's why animals are so stupid. The soul of an animal can split up and become, in its smallest division, an organism or plant. The feelings which plants have, then, are what separated from the animal's soul when it split up at death. Although the life force of a large number of plants may appear sizeable, it is not as great as that of a single animal or a single mouthful of meat. Take, for example, rice: Tens of billions of grains of rice do not contain as much life force as a single piece of meat. If you open your five eyes you can know this at a glance. If you haven't opened your eyes, no matter how one tries to explain it to you, you won't understand. No matter how it's explained, you won't believe it, because you haven't been a plant!

Another example is the mosquitoes. The millions of mosquitoes on this mountain may be simply the soul of one person which has transformed into all those bugs. It's not the case that a single human soul turns into a single mosquito. One person can turn into limitless, boundless numbers of mosquitoes.

At death, the nature changes, the soul scatters, and its smallest fragments become plants. Thus, there is a difference between eating plants and eating animals. What is more, plants have very short lifespans. The grass, for example, is born in the spring and dies within months. Animals live a long time. If you don't kill them, they'll live for many years. Rice, regardless of the conditions, will only live a short time. So, if you really look into it, there are many factors to consider, and even science hasn't got it straight.

Student: Do Buddhists have some way of counteracting the effects of eating meat on a karmic level?

The Master: The Buddha ate meat. But he did not kill the animals he ate. He condoned three kinds of pure meat which could be eaten by Bhikshus and lay people. What are the three kinds of pure meat?

> *If you did not see*
> *the animal killed, it is pure.*
> *If you did not hear its cries*
> *as it was being killed, it is pure.*
> *If it was not killed*
> *expressly for you, it is pure.*

If you didn't see the animal killed or hear its screams as it died, and if the animal wasn't killed just for you to eat, in that case, if your body is weak, you can eat it. In the Buddha's day, the monks went out begging for food and they ate whatever they were given. It wasn't that they wanted to eat a particular thing and so they cooked it. They just ate whatever was offered to them. If they were offered meat, they were allowed to eat it.

But why is it that cultivators of the Way should not eat meat? It's because eating meat increases people's sexual desire. Cultivators should have no sexual desire, and so they should consume food and drink which do not stimulate desire. That's the most important reason, really, for practicing vegetarianism. Cultivators must be pure and undefiled. That is the most important reason for not eating meat.

\* \* \*

The assembly then drove in a caravan to the ocean and performed the final Great Transference of Merit at the beach as the sun set, recalling the first of the contemplations listed in the *Sutra of Sixteen Contemplations*: "Contemplate the setting sun, its appearance like that of a suspended drum…"

A ceremony to transfer merit to the living and the dead was performed near the end of the week. Bhikshu Heng Su burns the memorial slips that people wrote on behalf of family and friends.

The falling rain, the gentle breeze, the very air itself — all express the Mahayana! Participants chant Amitabha Buddha's name while walking on a path beside the tent.

Amitabha Buddha's name echoes through the trees and up into the Oregon hills as participants chant in unison throughout the week-long session.

As the session progresses, more and more young Americans learn about the events taking place at Buddha Root Farm from their friends and relatives, so the line of chanters grows longer and the tent fills with meditators.

The misty rain doesn't stop cultivators from taking a walk while they chant. The group energy generated was mutually supportive and grew as the chanting of the Buddha's name continued day-by-day.

The Great Transference of Merit was performed each evening. Here, participants join in the grand finale, when Master Hua suggested everyone do the last Great Transference at the Oregon coast. Everyone is facing the West as the sun's rays sparkle on the ocean's waves.

Circumambulating while reciting the names of Amitabha Buddha, Guanyin and Great Strength Bodhisattva, and the Sea-like Assembly of Bodhisattvas in the Pure Land, everyone in the assembly is filled with joy and a sense of peace.

A spectacular finale! Transferring the merit of the week's practice of reciting Amitabha Buddha's name, everyone faces west as the waves roll in the golden sunset.

# Index

# 唵嘛呢叭嘧吽

## Om Mani Padme Hum

### Lecture given by Tripitaka Master Hsuan Hua

These six characters together make up the *Six Character Great Bright Mantra*; each one individually is able to emit brilliant light.

The first character is *nan* ( 唵, Sanskrit *om* ). When you recite "nan" once, all ghosts and spirits must place their palms together. Why do they put their palms together? To maintain the rules and regulations. Conforming to the regulations, they follow the correct way. Recite this one character and all ghosts and spirits do not dare rebel and create confusion; they do not dare disobey orders. This is the first sound in the Mantra.

"*Ma ni* ( 嘛呢, Sanskrit *mani* )" means "silent wisdom". Using wisdom one is able to understand all principles, and thus is able to be silently extinguished, without production. It is also defined as "separating from filth" which means leaving all dust and filth. It can be compared to the "precious as-you-will pearl" which is extremely pure, with no defilement. Whatever excellence you wish to bring forth, if you have the "precious as-you-wish pearl" it can be done. It can also fulfill your wishes in accord with your thoughts. Every vow you make will be fulfilled. These are its benefits.

"*Pa mi* ( 叭嘧, Sanskrit *padme* )" actually should read "*pa te mi* 叭嘧持". It means "light perfectly illuminating" and is also defined as "the opening of the lotus". It is analogous to the wonderful lotus flower which can complete, perfect and fulfill without obstruction. It is the wonderful mind of Avalokiteshvara Bodhisattva. This is "*pa mi*".

Next comes "*hung* ( 吽, Sanskrit: *hum* )" which means "put forth". Anything at all can be born from this character "hung". It also means "to protect and support". Recite this character and all Dharma protectors and good spirits come to support and protect you. It also means "eradicating disasters". Recite this character and whatever difficulties there are will be eradicated. It also means "success"; whatever you cultivate can be accomplished.

Recite the *Six Character Great Bright Mantra* once, and the immeasurable Buddhas, Bodhisattvas, and Vajra Dharma protectors constantly support and protect you. Therefore, when Avalokiteshvara Bodhisattva finished saying this *Six Character Great Bright Mantra*, there were seven million Buddhas who came to support, protect, and surround him. The strength and ability of the *Six Character Great Bright Mantra* are inconceivable, the intertwining of the response and way unimaginable, therefore it is called the Secret School. If one were to explain in detail, the meanings would be immeasurable and unlimited; they cannot be spoken completely.

# The Eighteen Great Vows of the Venerable Master Hua

1.  I vow that as long as there is a single Bodhisattva in the three periods of time throughout the ten directions of the Dharma Realm, to the very end of empty space, who has not accomplished Buddhahood, I too will not attain the right enlightenment.

2.  I vow that as long as there is a single Pratyekabuddha in the three periods of time throughout the ten directions of the Dharma Realm, to the very end of empty space, who has not accomplished Buddhahood, I too will not attain the right enlightenment.

3.  I vow that as long as there is a single Shravaka in the three periods of time throughout the ten directions of the Dharma Realm, to the very end of empty space, who has not accomplished Buddhahood, I too will not attain the right enlightenment.

4.  I vow that as long as there is a single god in the Triple Realm who has not accomplished Buddhahood, I too will not attain the right enlightenment.

5.  I vow that as long as there is a single human being in the worlds of the ten directions who has not accomplished Buddhahood, I too will not attain the right enlightenment.

6. I vow that as long as there is a single asura who has not accomplished Buddhahood, I too will not attain the right enlightenment.

7. I vow that as long as there is a single animal who has not accomplished Buddhahood, I too will not attain the right enlightenment.

8. I vow that as long as there is a single hungry ghost who has not accomplished Buddhahood, I too will not attain the right enlightenment.

9. I vow that as long as there is a single hell-dweller who has not accomplished Buddhahood, I too will not attain the right enlightenment.

10. I vow that as long as there is a single god, immortal, human, asura, air-bound or water-bound creature, animate or inanimate object, or a single dragon, beast, ghost, or spirit, and so forth, of the spiritual realm that has taken refuge with me and has not accomplished Buddhahood, I too will not attain the right enlightenment.

11. I vow to fully dedicate all blessings and bliss which I myself ought to receive and enjoy to all living beings of the Dharma Realm.

12. I vow to fully take upon myself all sufferings and hardships of all the living beings in the Dharma Realm.

13. I vow to manifest innumerable bodies as a means to gain access into the minds of living beings throughout the universe who do not believe in the Buddhadharma, causing them to correct their faults and tend toward wholesomeness, repent of their errors and start anew, take refuge in the Triple Jewel, and ultimately accomplish Buddhahood.

14. I vow that all living beings who see my face or even hear my name will fix their thoughts on Bodhi and quickly accomplish the Buddha Way.

15. I vow to respectfully observe the Buddha's instructions and cultivate the practice of eating only one meal per day.

16. I vow to enlighten all sentient beings, universally responding to the multitude of differing potentials.

17. I vow to obtain the five eyes, six spiritual powers, and the freedom of being able to fly in this very life.

18. I vow that all of my vows will certainly be fulfilled.


Conclusion:

*I vow to save the innumerable living beings.*
*I vow to eradicate the inexhaustible afflictions.*
*I vow to study the illimitable Dharma-doors.*
*I vow to accomplish the unsurpassed Buddha Way.*

# Buddhist Text Translation Society Publication

## Buddhist Text Translation Society
## International Translation Institute

http://www.bttsonline.org

1777 Murchison Drive,
Burlingame, California 94010-4504 USA
Phone: 650-692-5912 Fax: 650-692-5056

When Buddhism first came to China from India, one of the most important tasks required for its establishment was the translation of the Buddhist scriptures from Sanskrit into Chinese. This work involved a great many people, such as the renowned monk National Master Kumarajiva (fifth century), who led an assembly of over 800 people to work on the translation of the Tripitaka (Buddhist canon) for over a decade. Because of the work of individuals such as these, nearly the entire Buddhist Tripitaka of over a thousand texts exists to the present day in Chinese.

Now the banner of the Buddha's Teachings is being firmly planted in Western soil, and the same translation work is being done from Chinese into English. Since 1970, the Buddhist Text Translation Society (BTTS) has been making a paramount contribution toward this goal. Aware that the Buddhist Tripitaka is a work of such magnitude that its translation could never be entrusted to a single person, the BTTS, emulating the translation assemblies of ancient times, does not publish a work until it has passed through four committees for primary translation, revision, editing, and certification. The leaders of these committees are Bhikshus (monks) and Bhikshunis (nuns) who have devoted their lives to the study and practice of the Buddha's teachings. For this reason, all of the works of the BTTS put an emphasis on what the principles of the Buddha's teachings mean in terms of actual practice and not simply hypothetical conjecture.

The translations of canonical works by the Buddhist Text Translation Society are accompanied by extensive commentaries by the Venerable Tripitaka Master Hsuan Hua.

# BTTS Publications

**Buddhist Sutras.** Amitabha Sutra, Dharma Flower (Lotus) Sutra, Flower Adornment (Avatamsaka) Sutra, Heart Sutra & Verses without a Stand, Shurangama Sutra, Sixth Patriarch Sutra, Sutra in Forty-two Sections, Sutra of the Past Vows of Earth Store Bodhisattva, Vajra Prajna Paramita (Diamond) Sutra.

**Commentarial Literature.** Buddha Root Farm, City of 10 000 Buddhas Recitation Handbook, Filiality: The Human Source, Herein Lies the Treasure-trove, Listen to Yourself Think Everything Over, Shastra on the Door to Understanding the Hundred Dharmas, Song of Enlightenment, The Ten Dharma Realms Are Not Beyond a Single Thought, Venerable Master Hua's Talks on Dharma, Venerable Master Hua's Talks on Dharma during the 1993 Trip to Taiwan, Water Mirror Reflecting Heaven.

**Biographical.** In Memory of the Venerable Master Hsuan Hua, Pictorial Biography of the Venerable Master Hsü Yün, Records of High Sanghans, Records of the Life of the Venerable Master Hsüan Hua, Three Steps One Bow, World Peace Gathering, News from True Cultivators, Open Your Eyes Take a Look at the World, With One Heart Bowing to the City of 10 000 Buddhas.

**Children's Books.** Cherishing Life, Human Roots: Buddhist Stories for Young Readers, Spider Web, Giant Turtle, Patriarch Bodhidharma.

**Musics, Novels and Brochures.** Songs for Awakening, Awakening, The Three Cart Patriarch, City of 10 000 Buddhas Color Brochure, Celebrisi's Journey, Lots of Time Left.

**The Buddhist Monthly–Vajra Bodhi Sea** is a monthly journal of orthodox Buddhism which has been published by the Dharma Realm Buddhist Association, formerly known as the Sino-American Buddhist Association, since 1970. Each issue contains the most recent translations of the Buddhist canon by the Buddhist Text Translation Society. Also included in each issue are a biography of a great Patriarch of Buddhism from the ancient past, sketches of the lives of contemporary monastics and lay-followers around the world, articles on practice, and other material. The journal is bilingual, Chinese and English

Please visit our web-site at **www.bttsonline.org** for the latest publications and for ordering information.

# The Dharma Realm Buddhist Association

## Mission

The Dharma Realm Buddhist Association (formerly the Sino-American Buddhist Association) was founded by the Venerable Master Hsuan Hua in the United States of America in 1959. Taking the Dharma Realm as its scope, the Association aims to disseminate the genuine teachings of the Buddha throughout the world. The Association is dedicated to translating the Buddhist canon, propagating the Orthodox Dharma, promoting ethical education, and bringing benefit and happiness to all beings. Its hope is that individuals, families, the society, the nation, and the entire world will, under the transforming influence of the Buddhadharma, gradually reach the state of ultimate truth and goodness.

## The Founder

The Venerable Master, whose names were An Tse and To Lun, received the Dharma name Hsuan Hua and the transmission of Dharma from Venerable Master Hsu Yun in the lineage of the Wei Yang Sect. He was born in Manchuria, China, at the beginning of the century. At nineteen, he entered the monastic order and dwelt in a hut by his mother's grave to practice filial piety. He meditated, studied the teachings, ate only one meal a day, and slept sitting up. In 1948 he went to Hong Kong, where he established the Buddhist Lecture Hall and other Way-places. In 1962 he brought the Proper Dharma to the West, lecturing on several dozen Mahayana Sutras in the United States. Over the years, the Master established more than twenty monasteries of Proper Dharma under the auspices of the Dharma Realm Buddhist Association and the City of Ten Thousand Buddhas. He also founded centers for the translation of the Buddhist canon and for education to spread the influence of the Dharma in the East and West. The Master manifested the stillness in the United States in 1995. Through his lifelong, selfless dedication to teaching living beings with wisdom and compassion, he influenced countless people to change their faults and to walk upon the pure, bright path to enlightenment.

## Dharma Propagation, Buddhist Text Translation, and Education

The Venerable Master Hua's three great vows after leaving the home-life were (1) to propagate the Dharma, (2) to translate the Buddhist Canon, and (3) to promote education. In order to make these vows a reality, the Venerable Master based himself on the Three Principles and the Six Guidelines. Courageously facing every hardship, he founded monasteries, schools, and centers in the West, drawing in living beings and teaching them on a vast scale. Over the years, he founded the following institutions:

## The City of Ten Thousand Buddhas and Its Branches

In propagating the Proper Dharma, the Venerable Master not only trained people but also founded Way-places where the Dharma wheel could turn and living beings could be saved. He wanted to provide cultivators with pure places to practice in accord with the Buddha's regulations. Over the years, he founded many Way-places of Proper Dharma. In the United States and Canada, these include the City of Ten Thousand Buddhas; Gold Mountain Monastery; Gold Sage Monastery; Gold Wheel Monastery; Gold Summit Monastery; Gold Buddha Monastery; Avatamsaka Monastery; Long Beach Monastery; the City of the Dharma Realm; Berkeley Buddhist Monastery; Avatamsaka Hermitage; and Blessings, Prosperity, and Longevity Monastery. In Taiwan, there are the Dharma Realm Buddhist Books Distribution Association, Dharma Realm Monastery, and Amitabha Monastery. In Malaysia, there are the Prajna Guanyin Sagely Monastery (formerly Tze Yun Tung Temple), Deng Bi An Monastery, and Lotus Vihara. In Hong Kong, there are the Buddhist Lecture Hall and Cixing Monastery.

Purchased in 1974, the City of Ten Thousand Buddhas is the hub of the Dharma Realm Buddhist Association. The City is located in Talmage, Mendocino County, California, 110 miles north of San Francisco. Eighty of the 488 acres of land are in active use. The remaining acreage consists of meadows, orchards, and woods. With over seventy large buildings containing over 2,000 rooms, blessed with serenity and fresh, clean air, it is the first large Buddhist monastic community in the United States. It is also an international center for the Proper Dharma.

Although the Venerable Master Hua was the Ninth Patriarch in the Wei Yang Sect of the Chan School, the monasteries he founded emphasize all of the five main practices of Mahayana Buddhism (Chan meditation, Pure Land, esoteric, Vinaya (moral discipline), and doctrinal studies). This accords with the Buddha's words: "The Dharma is level and equal, with no high or low." At the City of Ten Thousand Buddhas, the rules of purity are rigorously observed. Residents of the City strive to regulate their own conduct and to cultivate with vigor. Taking refuge in the Proper Dharma, they lead pure and selfless lives, and attain peace in body and mind. The Sutras are expounded and the Dharma wheel is turned daily. Residents dedicate themselves wholeheartedly to making Buddhism flourish. Monks and nuns in all the monasteries take one meal a day, always wear their precept sash, and follow the Three Principles:

> *Freezing, we do not scheme.*
> *Starving, we do not beg.*
> *Dying of poverty, we ask for nothing.*
> *According with conditions, we do not change.*
> *Not changing, we accord with conditions.*
> *We adhere firmly to our three great principles.*
> *We renounce our lives to do the Buddha's work.*
> *We take the responsibility to mold our own destinies.*
> *We rectify our lives to fulfill the Sanghan's role.*
> *Encountering specific matters,*
>     *we understand the principles.*
> *Understanding the principles,*
>     *we apply them in specific matters.*
> *We carry on the single pulse of*
>     *the Patriarchs' mind-transmission.*

The monasteries also follow the Six Guidelines: not contending, not being greedy, not seeking, not being selfish, not pursuing personal advantage, and not lying.

---

## International Translation Institute

The Venerable Master vowed to translate the Buddhist Canon (Tripitaka) into Western languages so that it would be widely accessible throughout the world. In 1973, he founded the International Translation Institute on Washington Street in San Francisco for the purpose of translating Buddhist scriptures into English and other languages. In 1977, the Institute was merged into Dharma Realm Buddhist University as the Institute for the Translation of Buddhist Texts. In 1991, the Venerable Master purchased a large building in Burlingame (south of San Francisco) and established the International Translation Institute there for the purpose of translating and publishing Buddhist texts. To date, in addition to publishing over one hundred volumes of Buddhist texts in Chinese, the Association has published more than one hundred volumes of English, French, Spanish, Vietnamese, and Japanese translations of Buddhist texts, as well as bilingual (Chinese and English) editions. Audio and video tapes also continue to be produced. The monthly journal Vajra Bodhi Sea, which has been in circulation for nearly thirty years, has been published in bilingual (Chinese and English) format in recent years.

In the past, the difficult and vast mission of translating the Buddhist canon in China was sponsored and supported by the emperors and kings themselves. In our time, the Venerable Master encouraged his disciples to cooperatively shoulder this heavy responsibility, producing books and audio tapes and using the medium of language to turn the wheel of Proper Dharma and do the great work of the Buddha. All those who aspire to devote themselves to this work of sages should uphold the Eight Guidelines of the International Translation Institute:

1. One must free oneself from the motives of personal fame and profit.
2. One must cultivate a respectful and sincere attitude free from arrogance and conceit.
3. One must refrain from aggrandizing one's work and denigrating that of others.
4. One must not establish oneself as the standard of correctness and suppress the work of others with one's fault-finding.
5. One must take the Buddha-mind as one's own mind.
6. One must use the wisdom of Dharma-Selecting Vision to determine true principles.
7. One must request Virtuous Elders of the ten directions to certify one's translations.
8. One must endeavor to propagate the teachings by printing Sutras, Shastra texts, and Vinaya texts when the translations are certified as being correct.

These are the Venerable Master's vows, and participants in the work of translation should strive to realize them.

# Instilling Goodness Elementary School, Developing Virtue Secondary School, Dharma Realm Buddhist University

"Education is the best national defense." The Venerable Master Hua saw clearly that in order to save the world, it is essential to promote good education. If we want to save the world, we have to bring about a complete change in people's minds and guide them to cast out unwholesomeness and to pursue goodness. To this end the Master founded Instilling Goodness Elementary School in 1974, and Developing Virtue Secondary School and Dharma Realm Buddhist University in 1976.

In an education embodying the spirit of Buddhism, the elementary school teaches students to be filial to parents, the secondary school teaches students to be good citizens, and the university teaches such virtues as humaneness and righteousness. Instilling Goodness Elementary School and Developing Virtue Secondary School combine the best of contemporary and traditional methods and of Western and Eastern cultures. They emphasize moral virtue and spiritual development, and aim to guide students to become good and capable citizens who will benefit humankind. The schools offer a bilingual (Chinese/English) program where boys and girls study separately. In addition to standard academic courses, the curriculum includes ethics, meditation, Buddhist studies, and so on, giving students a foundation in virtue and guiding them to understand themselves and explore the truths of the universe. Branches of the schools (Sunday schools) have been established at branch monasteries with the aim of propagating filial piety and ethical education.

Dharma Realm Buddhist University, whose curriculum focuses on the Proper Dharma, does not merely transmit academic knowledge. It emphasizes a foundation in virtue, which expands into the study of how to help all living beings discover their inherent nature. Thus, Dharma Realm Buddhist University advocates a spirit of shared inquiry and free exchange of ideas, encouraging students to study various canonical texts and use different experiences and learning styles to tap their inherent wisdom and fathom the meanings of those texts. Students are encouraged to practice the principles they have understood and apply the Buddhadharma in their lives, thereby nurturing their wisdom and virtue. The University aims to produce outstanding individuals of high moral character who will be able to bring benefit to all sentient beings.

## Sangha and Laity Training Programs

In the Dharma-ending Age, in both Eastern and Western societies there are very few monasteries that actually practice the Buddha's regulations and strictly uphold the precepts. Teachers with genuine wisdom and understanding, capable of guiding those who aspire to pursue careers in Buddhism, are very rare. The Venerable Master founded the Sangha and Laity Training Programs in 1982 with the goals of raising the caliber of the Sangha, perpetuating the Proper Dharma, providing professional training for Buddhists around the world on both practical and theoretical levels, and transmitting the wisdom of the Buddha.

The Sangha Training Program gives monastics a solid foundation in Buddhist studies and practice, training them in the practical affairs of Buddhism and Sangha management. After graduation, students will be able to assume various responsibilities related to Buddhism in monasteries, institutions, and other settings. The program emphasizes a thorough knowledge of Buddhism, understanding of the scriptures, earnest cultivation, strict observance of precepts, and the development of a virtuous character, so that students will be able to propagate the Proper Dharma and perpetuate the Buddha's wisdom. The Laity Training Program offers courses to help laypeople develop correct views, study and practice the teachings, and understand monastic regulations and ceremonies, so that they will be able to contribute their abilities in Buddhist organizations.

## Let Us Go Forward Together

In this Dharma-ending Age when the world is becoming increasingly dangerous and evil, the Dharma Realm Buddhist Association, in consonance with its guiding principles, opens the doors of its monasteries and centers to those of all religions and nationalities. Anyone who is devoted to humaneness, righteousness, virtue, and the pursuit of truth, and who wishes to understand him or herself and help humankind, is welcome to come study and practice with us. May we together bring benefit and happiness to all living beings.

# Dharma Realm Buddhist Association Branches

### The City of Ten Thousand Buddhas
P.O. Box 217, Talmage, CA 95481-0217 USA
Tel: (707) 462-0939   Fax: (707) 462-0949
Home Page: http://www.drba.org

**Institute for World Religions (Berkeley Buddhist Monastery)**
2304 McKinley Avenue, Berkeley, CA 94703 USA
Tel: (510) 848-3440

**Dharma Realm Buddhist Books Distribution Society**
11th Floor, 85 Chung-hsiao E. Road, Sec. 6, Taipei, Taiwan R.O.C.
Tel: (02) 2786-3022   Fax: (02) 2786-2674

**The City of the Dharma Realm**
1029 West Capitol Avenue, West Sacramento, CA 95691 USA
Tel: (916) 374-8268

**Gold Mountain Monastery**
800 Sacramento Street, San Francisco, CA 94108 USA
Tel: (415) 421-6117   Fax: (415) 788-6001

**Gold Wheel Monastery**
235 North Avenue 58, Los Angeles, CA 90042 USA
Tel: (323) 258-6668

**Gold Buddha Monastery**
248 East 11th Avenue, Vancouver, B.C. V5T 2C3 Canada
Tel: (604) 709-0248   Fax: (604) 684-3754

**Gold Summit Monastery**
233 1st Avenue, West Seattle, WA 98119 USA
Tel: (206) 284-6690   Fax: (206) 284-6918

**Gold Sage Monastery**
11455 Clayton Road, San Jose, CA 95127 USA
Tel: (408) 923-7243   Fax: (408) 923-1064

**The International Translation Institute**
1777 Murchison Drive, Burlingame, CA 94010-4504 USA
Tel: (650) 692-5912   Fax: (650) 692-5056

**Long Beach Monastery**
3361 East Ocean Boulevard, Long Beach, CA 90803 USA
Tel: (562) 438-8902

**Blessings, Prosperity, & Longevity Monastery**
4140 Long Beach Boulevard, Long Beach, CA 90807 USA
Tel: (562) 595-4966

**Avatamsaka Hermitage**
11721 Beall Mountain Road, Potomac, MD 20854-1128 USA
Tel: (301) 299-3693

**Avatamsaka Monastery**
1009 4th Avenue, S.W. Calgary, AB T2P OK8 Canada
Tel: (403) 234-0644  Email: ava@nucleus.com

**Kun Yam Thong Temple**
161, Jalan Ampang, 50450 Kuala Lumpur, Malaysia
Tel: (03) 2164-8055  Fax: (03) 2163-7118

**Prajna Guanyin Sagely Monastery (formerly Tze Yun Tung)**
Batu 5½, Jalan Sungai Besi,
Salak Selatan, 57100 Kuala Lumpur, Malaysia
Tel: (03) 7982-6560  Fax: (03) 7980-1272

**Lotus Vihara**
136, Jalan Sekolah, 45600 Batang Berjuntai,
Selangor Darul Ehsan, Malaysia
Tel: (03) 3271-9439

**Buddhist Lecture Hall**
31 Wong Nei Chong Road, Top Floor, Happy Valley, Hong Kong, China
Tel: (02) 2572-7644

**Dharma Realm Sagely Monastery**
20, Tong-hsi Shan-chuang, Hsing-lung Village, Liu-kuei
Kaohsiung County, Taiwan, R.O.C.
Tel: (07) 689-3717  Fax: (07) 689-3870

**Amitabha Monastery**
7, Su-chien-hui, Chih-nan Village, Shou-feng,
Hualien County, Taiwan, R.O.C.
Tel: (07) 865-1956  Fax: (07) 865-3426

# Verse of Transference

May the merit and virtue accrued from this work,
Adorn the Buddhas' Pure Lands,
Repaying four kinds of kindness above,
And aiding those suffering in the paths below.

May those who see and hear of this,
All bring forth the resolve for Bodhi,
And when this retribution body is over,
Be born together in the Land of Ultimate Bliss.

Dharma Protector Wei Tuo Bodhisattva